USE YOUR LOAF

A Book of Bread Recipes
Old and New
compiled and edited
by Ursel Norman

With drawings
and step-by-step illustrations
by Derek Norman

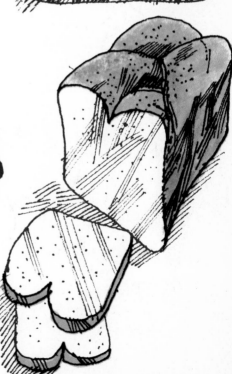

Fontana/Collins

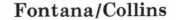

For Omi and Opa, Nana and Grandad

First published by William Collins Sons & Co. Ltd, Glasgow, 1974
First published in Fontana 1976
Copyright © Derek and Ursel Norman 1974

Made and printed in Great Britain by William Collins Sons & Co. Ltd, Glasgow

Use your Loaf is Ursel and Derek Norman's first book. In it they have combined their respective talents to produce an unusual collection of home-tested bread recipes. Their second book, *Salad Days*, is also available in Fontana.

Ursel was born in West Germany, and since her marriage has lived in London and Chicago. She is one of today's liberated women who thoroughly enjoys her job as a housewife and mother to three small children – Julia, Marcus and Carl. Making bread began as a means of escape from the characterless, shop-bought variety and has become a relaxing hobby which is greatly appreciated by her growing family. She also finds time for reading, studying languages and collecting antiques.

Derek Norman comes from Shropshire. He is a graduate of Chester School of Art, and while there he won the Caldecott Memorial Prize and spent a year as an exchange student at Central Michigan University, USA. Since then, he has worked in advertising in Britain and America and won awards in both countries. Besides sharing Ursel's love of good food, he enjoys painting and drawing, playing tennis, and collecting butterflies and children's books.

They have also published *Pasta and Oodles of Noodles* (Collins) and a new book, *Soup, Beautiful Soup* (Collins) is on the way.

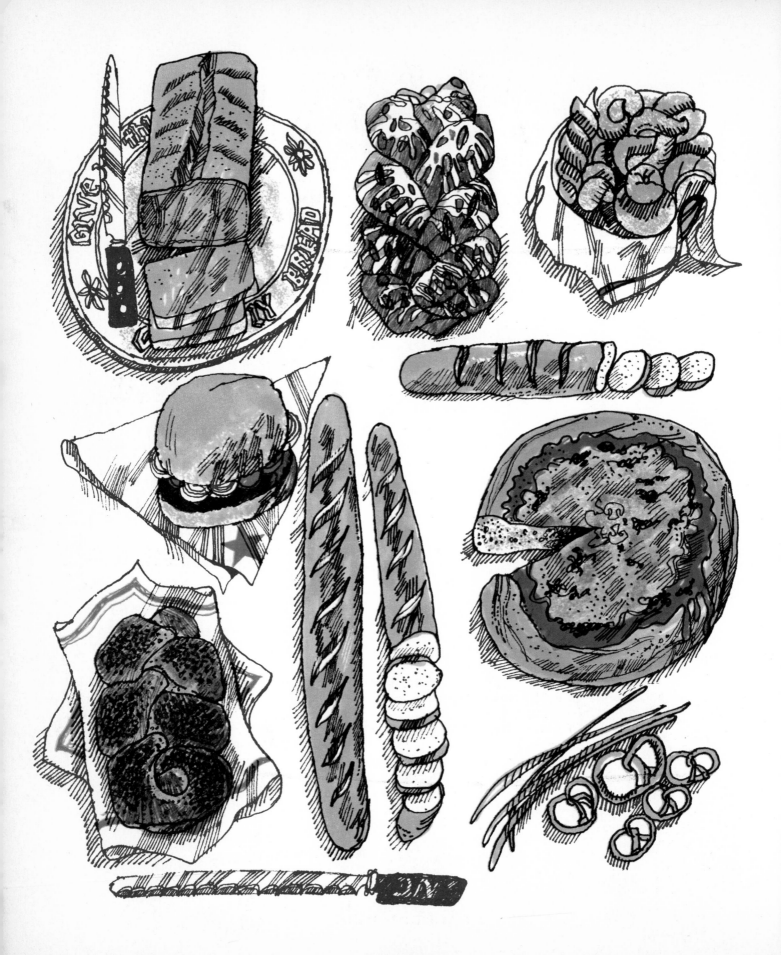

Contents

Introduction   page 6
How to Use your Loaf   8
The Old English Farmhouse Loaf   10
The French Loaf   12
The Cottage Loaf   14
Dinner Rolls   16
Grandmama's Milk Bread   18
The French Country Loaf   20
Poppy Seed Bread   22
Monastery Oatmeal Bread   24
The Vienna Loaf   26
Pumpernickel – Chicago Style   28
Country Oatmeal Rye   30
Yankee Buttermilk Rolls   32
Cheese Bread   34
The All-american Hamburger   36
Westphalian Sour Dough Rye   38
North of the Border Oatmeal Rolls   40
Pizza   42
Croissants   44
Brioches   46
Old English Herb Bread   48
Harvest Festival Raisin Bread   50
Viennese Gugelhupf   52
Chelsea Buns   54
Bara Brith   56
Danish Pastries   58
Salzstangen and Bretzeln   60
Index   63

Introduction

Like most people, I had always accepted the inevitability of buying shop bread. Certainly its convenience was beyond doubt, but the deteriorating quality and diminishing lack of choice gave rise to the question: Why don't I bake our own bread?

The case for baking our bread was further strengthened by the fact that my husband, myself and three small children were living in Chicago, USA, at the time, and the bread there is generally a good deal worse than in England. Nevertheless, all the signs are that the situation in England is getting to be much the same as in America.

So I started baking my own bread. Right from the beginning I found it easier and infinitely more enjoyable than I had been led to believe. So many people are under the impression that bread is unimaginative, comes in limited shapes and sizes and is generally white. This in fact is far from the truth, and it is hoped that the recipes shown and illustrated throughout this book will give a clue to the infinite variety of delicious breads that can be made. You will certainly not find many of them at your local supermarket, and most probably not even at your local baker (if one still exists), for in many cases I have resurrected older recipes which for varying reasons have been forgotten or fallen out of favour.

It still seems a luxury to have hot rolls for breakfast, croissants on Sunday morning, and warm, incredibly crusty bread to pass around at dinner parties. The smell of bread baking in the kitchen is always a great joy to the children when they come home from school; warm bread thickly spread with butter and honey is much more satisfying and nourishing than biscuits or buns.

Home-baked bread is not actually cheaper than bread bought in the shops, although buying large bags of flour makes it more economical; the end results however, are beyond comparison. Where can you buy brown, wholemeal bread, packed full of nourishment and with a truly crisp crust? Dinner rolls in different fancy shapes? Honest-to-goodness milk bread? Bread with oats added? (Oats must be the most nourishing cereal of all.) A juicy authentic Italian pizza, big enough for a buffet party? Real sour-dough bread of any kind? Our book has been designed to give you this kind of choice.

All the recipes, you will find, are basically simple and very easy to follow. It is hoped that the introduction to each bread will give you a clue as to its origin, what it goes best with, and the kind of taste to expect.

Designing this book and compiling and editing the recipes has been a labour of love. We have tried to make it very easy to use and understand, and we hope the drawings and writing convey some of the fun of baking bread.

Once over the initial hurdles of doubt and hesitation, this book will make baking bread a source of continuing satisfaction, to you, your family, and your guests.

Bon appétit!

Ursel Norman
Derek Norman

London 1973

How to Use Your Loaf.
The Do's & Don'ts

To avoid anxiety about yeast doughs, which are often thought of as being very fragile, it is necessary to understand just how yeast works. Once this is understood, the whole process of bread baking will be quite easy.

The Yeast

Yeast is a form of living plant. In order to reproduce, it needs a little sugar to feed on, and moisture and warmth in which to develop. Excessive amounts of sugar or heat will kill the yeast, while too low a temperature will slow the growth down to a minimum; excessive draughts therefore should be avoided. The natural sugar contents in the ingredients are usually sufficient to activate fresh yeast, but with dried yeast it is safer to add one teaspoon of sugar. To cream 1 teaspoon of dried yeast or an ounce of fresh yeast, sprinkle it onto $\frac{1}{4}$ pint lukewarm water or milk. The amount of yeast for each pound of flour is: up to 1 lb, $\frac{1}{2}$ oz; from 1 lb to 7 lbs, 1 oz. You will probably never have to use more than 1 oz at a time.

Fresh yeast, easily obtainable at Health Shops, can be stored for about a week in a covered container in a refrigerator. Dried yeast does not require refrigeration – it will keep for months in a tin with a tight fitting lid – but dried yeast does not seem to give quite such satisfactory results as fresh.

Kneading

Kneading is a very important part of bread baking. It is best done by hand on a flat surface for the yeast to be mixed thoroughly which is vital for even rising. The dough should be punched and pulled and slapped onto the table repeatedly to ensure proper mixing. If the dough seems sticky at this point, flour your hands, *never the table or the dough*. Be careful not to flour too much, as the dough must always remain soft and elastic. Kneading also brings out the gluten content in the flour, which finally gives the dough its elasticity.

Rising

After kneading, the dough must always be left to rise. Put it in a bowl covered with a damp cloth (to stop a crust forming) until the dough has doubled in size. This will ensure even distribution of all the ingredients; lumps of yeast left in the dough make it quite unpalatable.

Knocking Back

After the dough has risen it must always be brought back to its original size by knocking back. The dough is kneaded with the hands for a few minutes to avoid excessive air bubbles in the bread.

Proving

To make absolutely sure that all the ingredients are evenly distributed and the bread of a good texture, all loaves must be left – covered – to double in volume again before going into the oven.

Baking

All bread has to go into a very hot oven for the first 15–20 minutes of baking time. This is to kill the yeast to avoid excessive rising.

Testing

To test whether bread is baked tap the bottom. If it sounds quite hollow, the bread is done.

Re-heating

All breads or rolls, with the exception of sweet ones with icings or glazes, can be re-heated very satisfactorily. Sprinkle a few drops of water onto the oven floor to replace any moisture lost through re-heating, storing or freezing, and place the loaf in a very hot oven for 10–15 minutes. This is a good trick for dinner parties: fresh crusty bread can be baked up to 2–3 days in advance, and reheated.

Finishing Touches

For a finishing touch there are a number of glazes which can be brushed over the shaped dough before, during or even after baking. Rolls must be brushed gently *before* baking since they require very little oven time, but breads which are in the oven for an hour or more tend to get too brown if brushed beforehand, and have a more appetizing appearance if brushed about 20 minutes before they are ready.

Use cream, top of the milk, or evaporated milk for a shiny, yellow finish; beaten egg if you prefer the appearance to be really glossy; or salt water if you want your crust very crisp. Melted butter brushed on top of the loaf gives it a more matt finish, and highlights the colour beautifully, but it must be brushed on after baking, while the bread is still hot.

The same applies to sweet glazes being used on hot breads or buns, although icings can only be applied to cold buns, or the icing sugar will melt and run off.

French loaves are excellent made into garlic bread. Cut a finished loaf into thick slices, being careful not to cut through the bottom, and spread all the slices on both sides thickly with softened butter, creamed with a crushed clove or two of garlic. Try using a teaspoon of mixed herbs or finely minced onion instead of garlic to ring the changes. Then wrap the whole loaf in foil and heat it in a hot oven for about 20 minutes.

These are some quite sound facts about yeast cookery, but in the course of baking you will acquire your own little ways of doing things: the ways which work best for you. There are no hard and fast rules; yeast keeps on working for several hours, so just take things slowly.

Try it – you may surprise yourself!

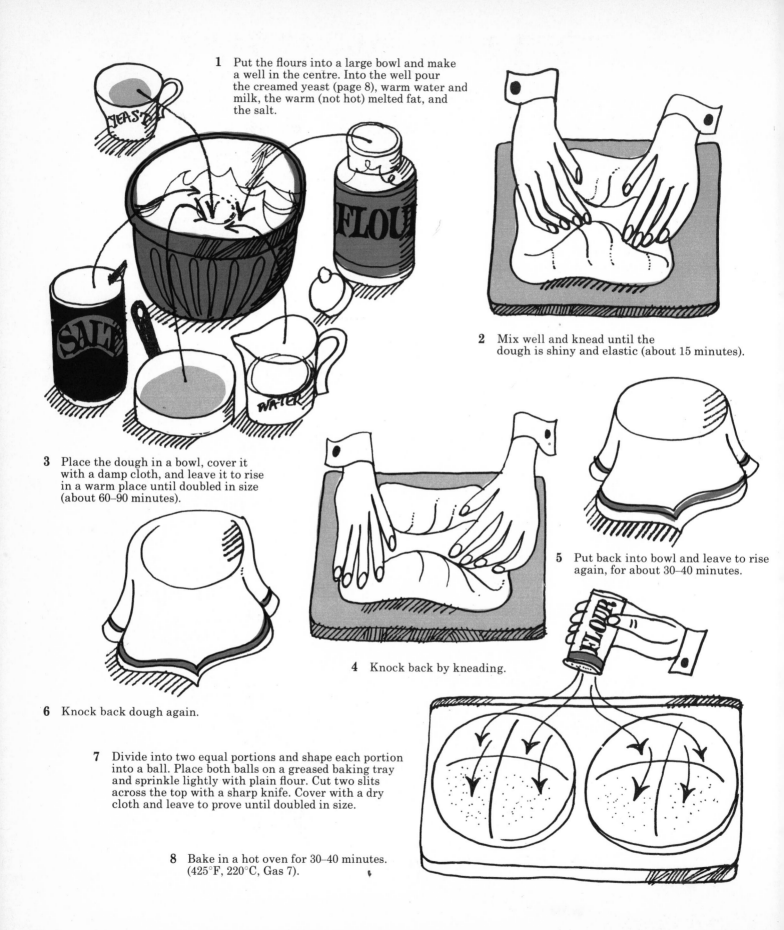

1 Put the flours into a large bowl and make a well in the centre. Into the well pour the creamed yeast (page 8), warm water and milk, the warm (not hot) melted fat, and the salt.

FLOUR

SALT

WATER

2 Mix well and knead until the dough is shiny and elastic (about 15 minutes).

3 Place the dough in a bowl, cover it with a damp cloth, and leave it to rise in a warm place until doubled in size (about 60–90 minutes).

5 Put back into bowl and leave to rise again, for about 30–40 minutes.

4 Knock back by kneading.

6 Knock back dough again.

7 Divide into two equal portions and shape each portion into a ball. Place both balls on a greased baking tray and sprinkle lightly with plain flour. Cut two slits across the top with a sharp knife. Cover with a dry cloth and leave to prove until doubled in size.

FLOUR

8 Bake in a hot oven for 30–40 minutes. (425°F, 220°C, Gas 7).

THE OLD ENGLISH FARMHOUSE LOAF

This loaf has a real country character. Wheat-brown in appearance, with a country texture and crisp fresh crust, it tastes great with a bowl of soup or creamy hors d'oeuvres.

To make 2 loaves

$1\frac{1}{2}$ lb ($\frac{2}{3}$ kg) wholemeal flour
$1\frac{1}{2}$ lb ($\frac{2}{3}$ kg) plain white flour
1 oz (30 gm) fresh yeast

pinch of sugar
1 pint ($\frac{1}{2}$ litre) warm water
$\frac{1}{2}$ pint ($\frac{1}{4}$ litre) warm milk
1 oz (30 gm) melted fat
2 teaspoons salt

1   Cream the yeast and sugar with 2 fl oz warm water.

2   Pour warm milk, 4 fl oz water and salt into a bowl.

3   Stir in the yeast mixture
and slowly add the flour, a little at a time.
Mix with a wooden spoon until the mixture
becomes a medium firm dough.

5   Place the dough in a bowl, cover with a damp
cloth and leave to rise in a warm place
until double in size (about 60 minutes).
Knock back, leave to rise for about 40 minutes.

4   Knead well on a lightly floured surface,
for at least 10 minutes. Sprinkle the surface
with more flour if the dough becomes sticky.

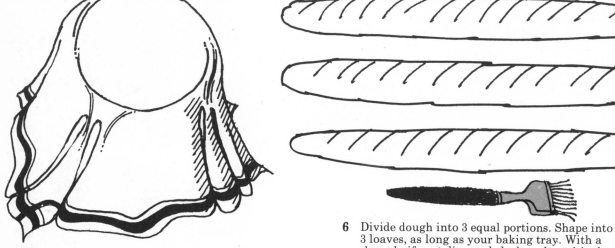

7   Dissolve salt in warm water
and brush glaze onto loaves.
Let the loaves rise until
double in bulk.

6   Divide dough into 3 equal portions. Shape into
3 loaves, as long as your baking tray. With a
sharp knife cut diagonal slashes about $\frac{1}{2}$ inch
deep at 2 inch intervals on top of the loaves.

8   Place baking tray (with loaves) in the oven. On rack beneath baking tray, place
another baking tray filled with water. Bake in a pre-heated oven (425°F, 220°C or
Gas 7) for 15 minutes. Reduce heat to 375°F, 190°C, Gas 5, brushing loaves again
with salt solution. Repeat after 10 minutes. Bake another 15–20 minutes, till crisp
and golden. Remove from oven and cool on a wire tray.

The French Loaf

The basic French loaf, crisp and full-bodied,
is as essential to a Frenchman's table
as a glass of wine.
Try it with a chunk of Cheddar
and a glass of beer.

To make 3 loaves,
about 15 inches long

1 oz (30 gm) fresh yeast
1 teaspoon sugar
2 fl oz (55 ml) warm water
12 fl oz (325 ml) warm milk
4 fl oz (110 ml) warm water
2 teaspoons salt
2 lb (1 kg) plain flour
1 teaspoon salt   } for
4 fl oz (110 ml) water } brushing

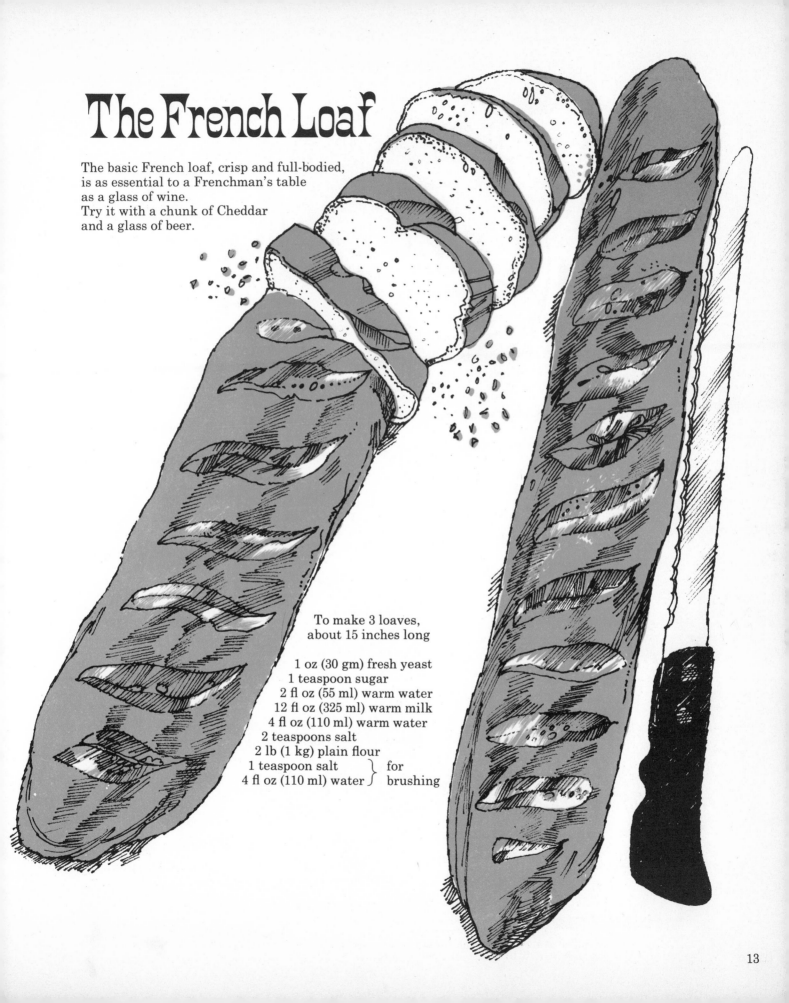

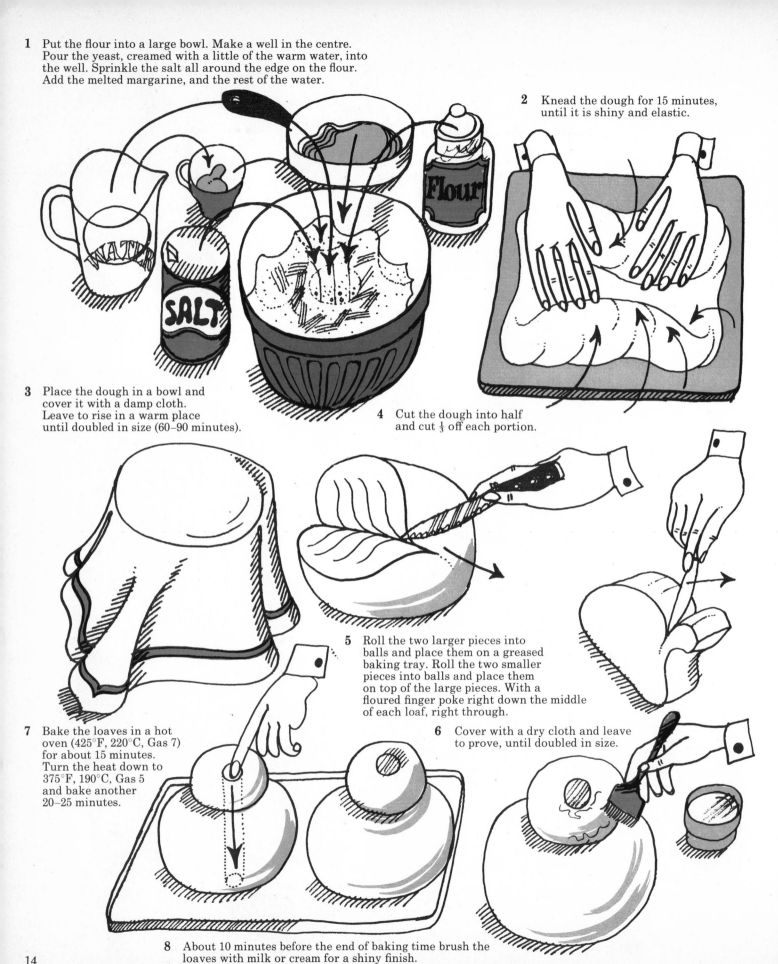

1 Put the flour into a large bowl. Make a well in the centre. Pour the yeast, creamed with a little of the warm water, into the well. Sprinkle the salt all around the edge on the flour. Add the melted margarine, and the rest of the water.

2 Knead the dough for 15 minutes, until it is shiny and elastic.

3 Place the dough in a bowl and cover it with a damp cloth. Leave to rise in a warm place until doubled in size (60–90 minutes).

4 Cut the dough into half and cut ⅓ off each portion.

5 Roll the two larger pieces into balls and place them on a greased baking tray. Roll the two smaller pieces into balls and place them on top of the large pieces. With a floured finger poke right down the middle of each loaf, right through.

7 Bake the loaves in a hot oven (425°F, 220°C, Gas 7) for about 15 minutes. Turn the heat down to 375°F, 190°C, Gas 5 and bake another 20–25 minutes.

6 Cover with a dry cloth and leave to prove, until doubled in size.

8 About 10 minutes before the end of baking time brush the loaves with milk or cream for a shiny finish.

14

THE COTTAGE LOAF

Try this old English recipe for wholemeal bread, pure and
simple – full of country character and wholehearted goodness.
It goes well with good conversation, a little Stilton
cheese and a glass of port.

To make 2 loaves

2½ lb (1¼ kg) stoneground
   wholemeal flour
1 oz (30 gm) fresh yeast

about 2 pints (1¼ litres)
   warm water
2 teaspoons salt
2 oz (55 gm) melted
   margarine

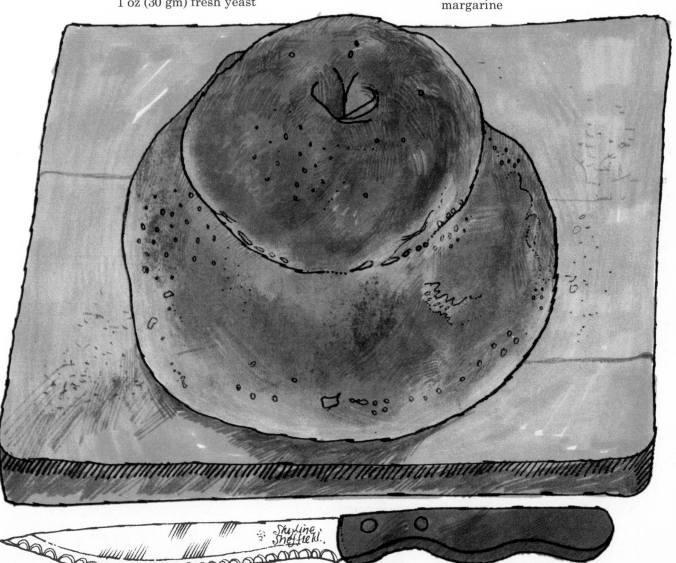

1 Sieve the flour into a bowl and make a well in the centre. Into the well crumble the yeast, the sugar and a little milk. Mix with some of the flour to a creamy consistency.

2 Onto the edge of the flour, put small slices of margarine and the salt (don't let the salt touch the yeast, for this slows down fermentation to a minimum).

3 Cover with a dry cloth and leave to ferment for 10 minutes.

4 Add the rest of the milk and knead to a soft, smooth dough.

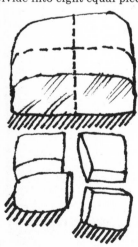

5 Knead for 10–15 minutes. Leave to rise, covered with a damp cloth, for about 1 hour. Knock back by kneading.

6 Divide into eight equal pieces.

7 Knead each piece well and mould into different fancy shapes.

8 Cover with a dry cloth and leave to prove on a baking tray for 30–40 minutes. Then brush gently with beaten egg and sprinkle with poppy seeds.

9 Bake in a hot oven (425°F, 220°C, Gas 7) for about 12 minutes.

DINNER ROLLS

These beautiful white dinner
rolls, with soft golden crusts, are
pure and fine in texture, delicious with
fresh butter, and a superb prelude to a meal.
They are delicately shaped and elegant enough to
grace any dinner table.

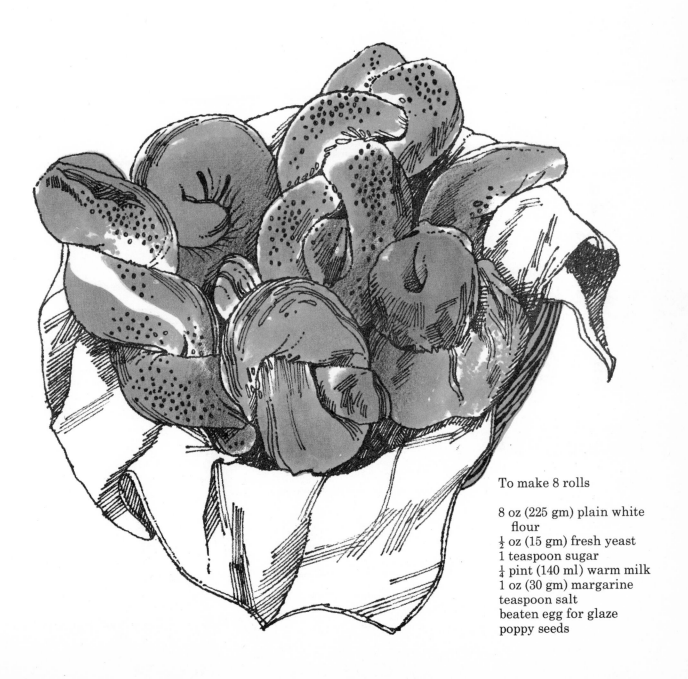

To make 8 rolls

8 oz (225 gm) plain white
   flour
½ oz (15 gm) fresh yeast
1 teaspoon sugar
¼ pint (140 ml) warm milk
1 oz (30 gm) margarine
teaspoon salt
beaten egg for glaze
poppy seeds

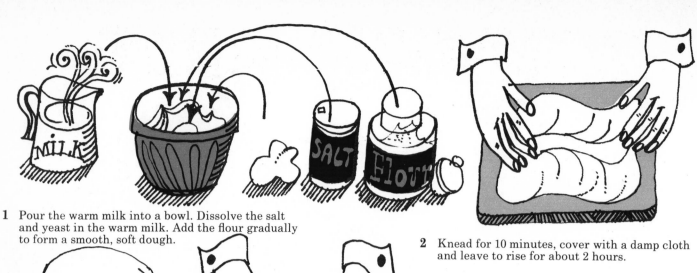

1 Pour the warm milk into a bowl. Dissolve the salt and yeast in the warm milk. Add the flour gradually to form a smooth, soft dough.

2 Knead for 10 minutes, cover with a damp cloth and leave to rise for about 2 hours.

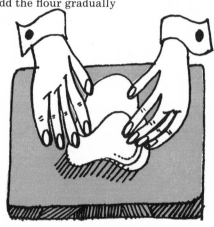

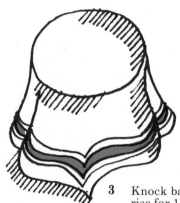

4 Knock back again and cut into two pieces.

3 Knock back and leave to rise for 1 hour further.

5 Divide each piece into three then roll these pieces into 15-inch long sausages. Dampen the ends to stick them together and plait.

6 Place each plait in a greased tin. Cover with a dry cloth and prove until doubled in size.

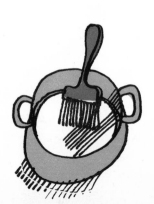

7 Bake in a hot oven (425°F, 220°C, Gas 7) for about 40 minutes. During the last 10 minutes of baking time brush the loaves with beaten egg for a glossy finish.

GRANDMAMA'S MILK BREAD

A beautiful Victorian bread, white and delicate in taste and texture, Grandmama's Milk Bread is a favourite with children, and makes excellent sandwiches and toast.

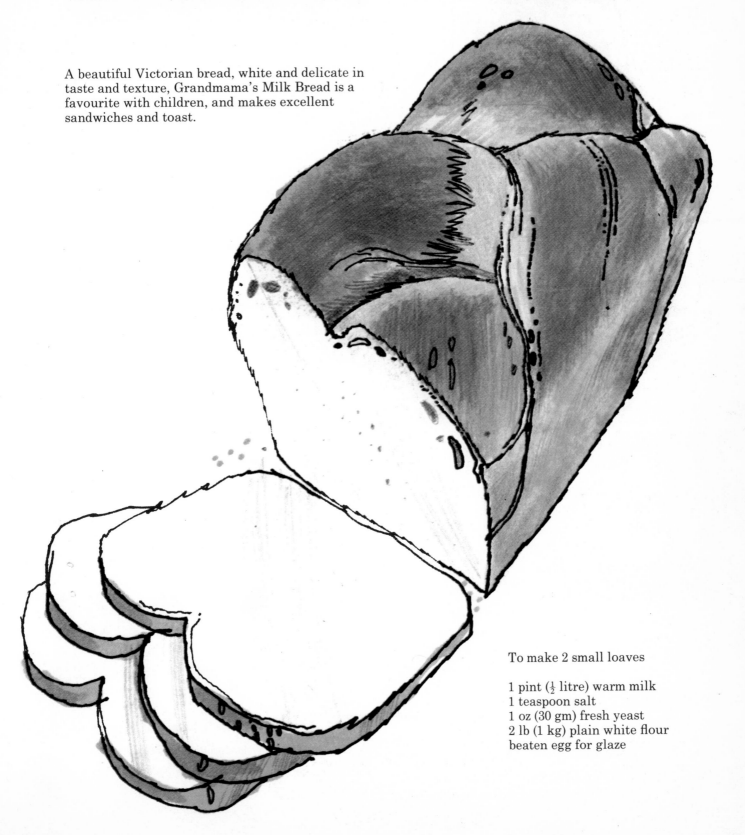

To make 2 small loaves

1 pint (½ litre) warm milk
1 teaspoon salt
1 oz (30 gm) fresh yeast
2 lb (1 kg) plain white flour
beaten egg for glaze

FIRST STAGE

1 Empty the flour into a bowl and make a well in the centre. Cream the yeast with some of the warm water and pour it into the well. Add the rest of the water.

2 Mix well and knead to a smooth dough.

3 Cover with a dry towel and leave to rise for 3–4 hours, or overnight.

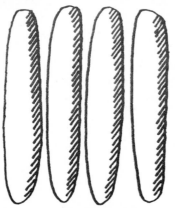

2 Gradually add the flour.

3 Knead for about 15 minutes.

SECOND STAGE

1 Dissolve the salt in warm water. Pour it over the dough, (which is now covered by a crusty skin). Mix well until the skin has disappeared.

4 Cover the dough with a damp cloth and leave to rise for at least another 2 hours.

5 Divide the dough into four equal portions. Shape each piece into a ball and leave to rise, covered with a dry towel, for about 15 minutes.

6 Roll each ball into a sausage shaped loaf, as long as your baking tray.

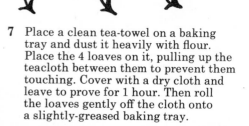

8 Make a few shallow cuts across each loaf with a sharp knife.

7 Place a clean tea-towel on a baking tray and dust it heavily with flour. Place the 4 loaves on it, pulling up the teacloth between them to prevent them touching. Cover with a dry cloth and leave to prove for 1 hour. Then roll the loaves gently off the cloth onto a slightly-greased baking tray.

9 Bake in a hot oven (425°F, 220°C, Gas 7) for about 1 hour. After the first half hour, brush the loaves with milk or cream.

The French Country Loaf

This crusty favourite of Provincial France is firm and even textured, allowing even and easy cutting. It's great for picnics and country cookouts. Try it with a chunk of cheese and a glass of red wine.

To make 4 loaves

FIRST STAGE	SECOND STAGE
1 lb ($\frac{1}{2}$ kg) plain white flour	$\frac{1}{2}$ oz (15gm) salt
1 oz (30 gm) fresh yeast	$\frac{1}{2}$ pint ($\frac{1}{4}$ litre) warm water
$\frac{1}{4}$ pint (140 ml) warm water	1 lb ($\frac{1}{2}$ kg) plain white flour

1 Dissolve the yeast and sugar in some of the milk. Leave to ferment for a few minutes.

2 Add the beaten egg, remaining milk and melted margarine salt and enough flour to make a soft dough.

3 Knead for 10 minutes.

4 Leave to rise, covered with a damp cloth, for 30–40 minutes.

5 Knock back by kneading.

6 Leave to rise again, covered with a damp cloth.

7 Knock back again.

8 Divide into three equal pieces. Roll each piece into a long sausage shape and plait these together loosely. Place on a greased baking tray and leave to prove, covered with a dry cloth, for 40–50 minutes.

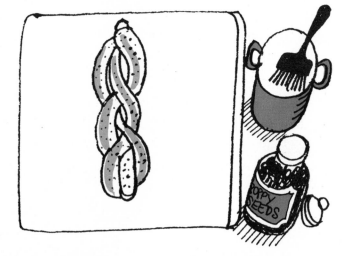

9 Brush carefully with beaten egg and sprinkle heavily with poppy seeds.

10 Bake in a hot oven (400°F, 200°C, Gas 6) for 30 minutes.

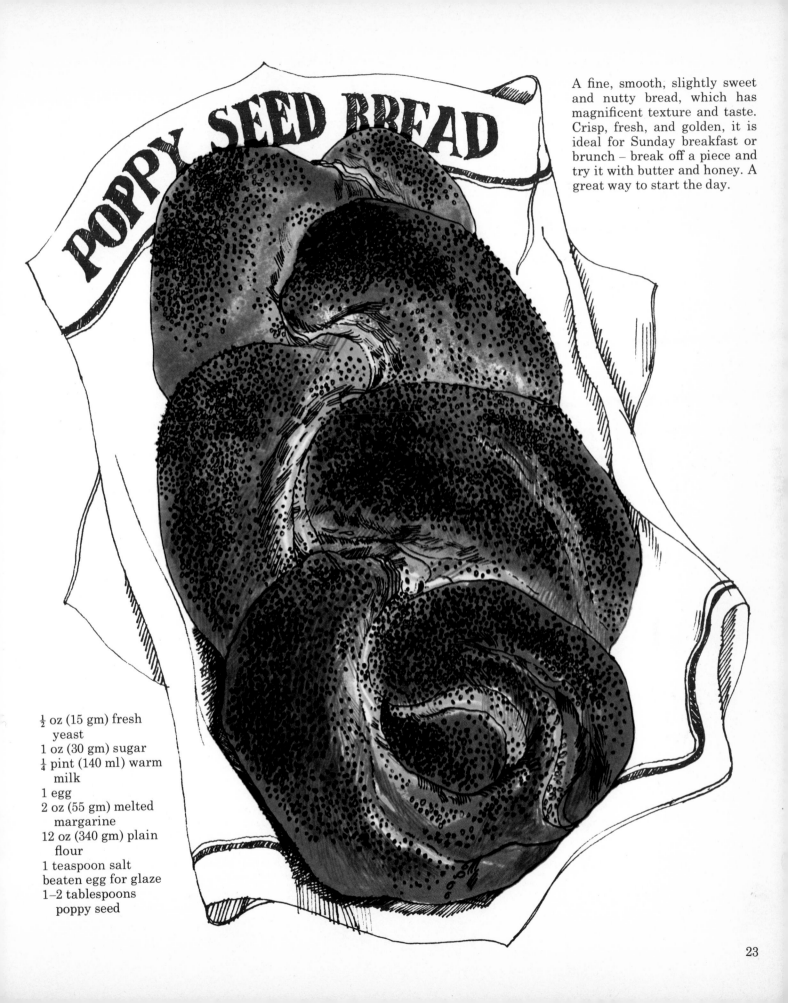

POPPY SEED BREAD

A fine, smooth, slightly sweet and nutty bread, which has magnificent texture and taste. Crisp, fresh, and golden, it is ideal for Sunday breakfast or brunch – break off a piece and try it with butter and honey. A great way to start the day.

$\frac{1}{2}$ oz (15 gm) fresh
    yeast
1 oz (30 gm) sugar
$\frac{1}{4}$ pint (140 ml) warm
    milk
1 egg
2 oz (55 gm) melted
    margarine
12 oz (340 gm) plain
    flour
1 teaspoon salt
beaten egg for glaze
1–2 tablespoons
    poppy seed

1   Dissolve the yeast and sugar in the milk.

2   Put white and wholemeal flours into a bowl.

3   Add the yeast mixture to the flour and stir well with a spoon.

4   Leave to rise, covered with a damp cloth, for 1 hour.

SECOND STAGE

1   Add the salt, melted margarine, wholemeal flour and oats, and knead to a fairly soft dough for about 15 minutes. Leave to rise, covered with a damp cloth, for 50 minutes.

2   Knock back by kneading. Leave to rise again, for about 40 minutes. Knock back again.

3   Shape into 2 loaves and put them into greased baking tins. Cut diagonal lines across the top with a sharp knife.

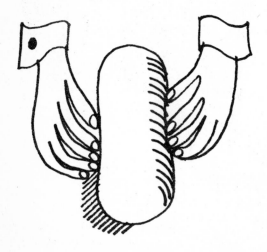

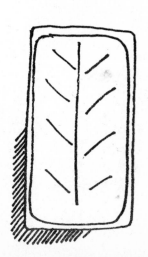

4   Leave to prove until double in size, about 1 hour. Bake in hot oven (425°F, 220°C, Gas 7) for about 1 hour.

Monastery Oatmeal Bread.

This rustic textured, chewy bread is wholesome, crusty, and packed full of goodness, and delicious for breakfast, or afternoon tea. Try it with a little honey, or, if the mood takes you, with a glass of wine.

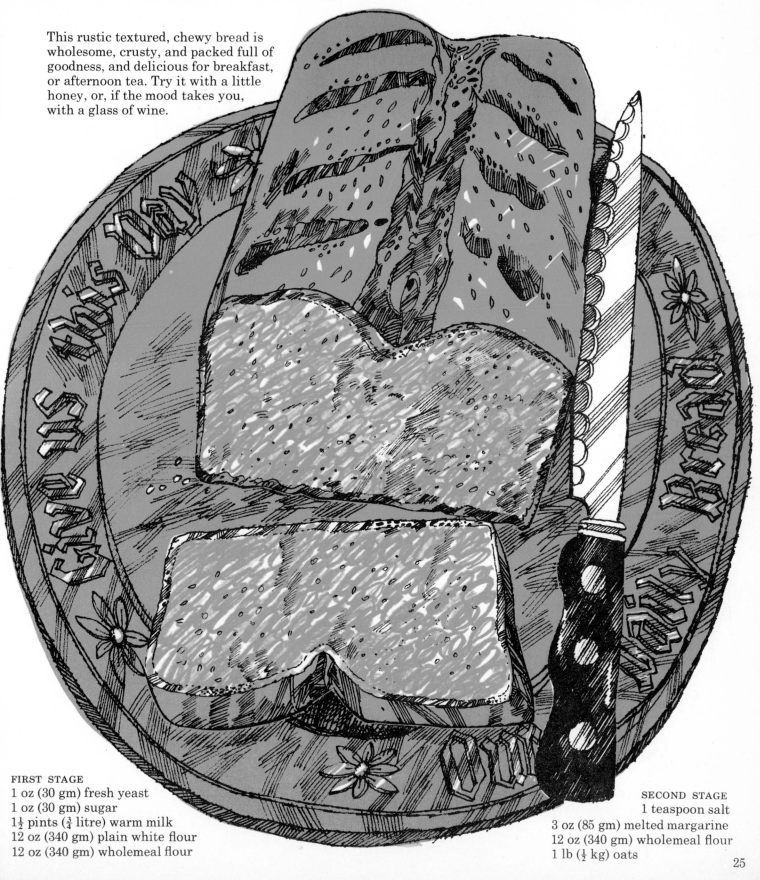

FIRST STAGE
1 oz (30 gm) fresh yeast
1 oz (30 gm) sugar
1½ pints (¾ litre) warm milk
12 oz (340 gm) plain white flour
12 oz (340 gm) wholemeal flour

SECOND STAGE
1 teaspoon salt
3 oz (85 gm) melted margarine
12 oz (340 gm) wholemeal flour
1 lb (½ kg) oats

1 Put the flour into a bowl and make a well in the centre. Sprinkle the salt around the edge of the well. Into the well pour the yeast (creamed with a little of the warm milk), the melted (not hot) butter, the rest of the milk and, if needed, some warm water.

2 Mix well and knead until a medium firm dough is formed, about 10–15 minutes.

3 Leave to rise in the bowl, covered with a damp cloth, for 60–90 minutes.

4 Knock back the dough by kneading.

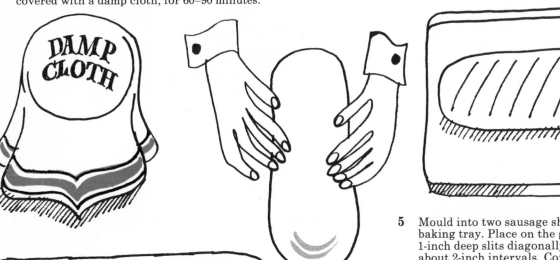

5 Mould into two sausage shapes as long as your baking tray. Place on the greased tray and cut 1-inch deep slits diagonally across the top, at about 2-inch intervals. Cover with a dry cloth and leave to prove in a warm place until doubled in size.

6 Bake in a hot oven (425°F, 220°C, Gas 7) for 20 minutes, then brush the loaves with milk or cream and, if you wish, sprinkle with poppy seeds. Put back in a cooler oven (375°F, 190°C, Gas 5) for about 30 minutes longer.

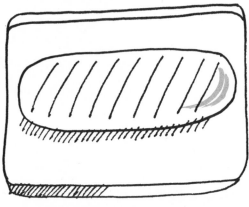

VIENNA BREAD

This Viennese favourite is a simple loaf, with a refined and subtle texture; soft and delicate with a rich golden crust. Try it with Wiener Schnitzel and a glass of beer.

To make 2 large loaves

2½ lb (1¼ kg) plain white flour
2 teaspoons salt
1 oz (30 gm) fresh yeast
1 pint (½ litre) warm milk
4 oz (110 gm) melted
butter or margarine
milk or cream
poppy seed

1 Dissolve the yeast in the water.

2 Heat the milk and melt the margarine in it. Allow to cool until it is lukewarm. Stir in the molasses, beaten egg, salt and yeast mixture. Add ½ lb rye flour and the caraway seeds and beat until smooth. Leave to rise for ½ hour.

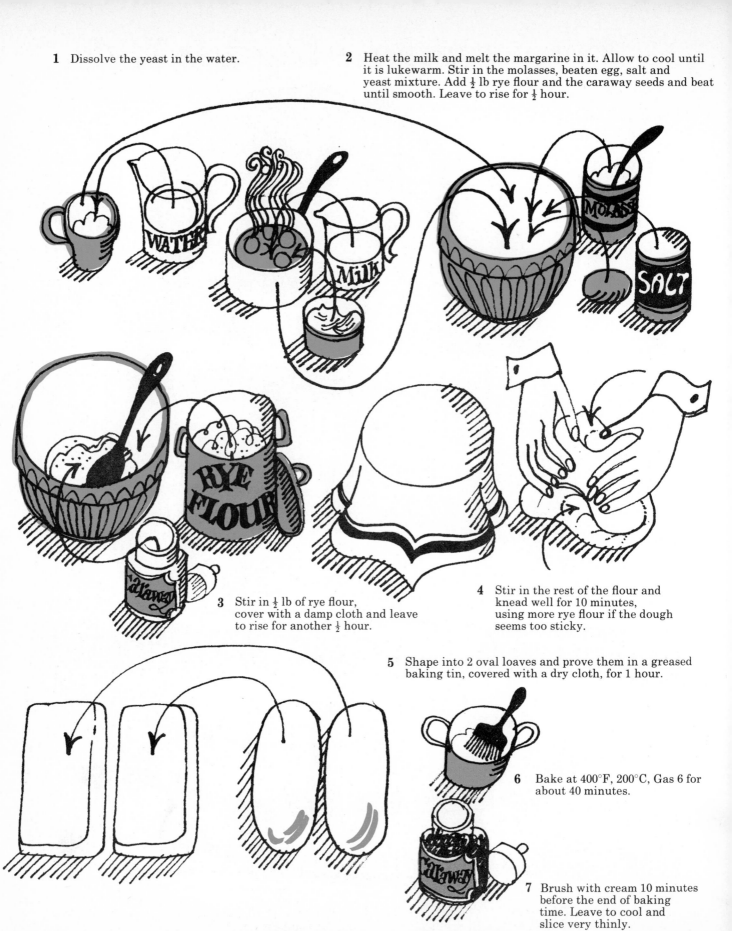

3 Stir in ½ lb of rye flour, cover with a damp cloth and leave to rise for another ½ hour.

4 Stir in the rest of the flour and knead well for 10 minutes, using more rye flour if the dough seems too sticky.

5 Shape into 2 oval loaves and prove them in a greased baking tin, covered with a dry cloth, for 1 hour.

6 Bake at 400°F, 200°C, Gas 6 for about 40 minutes.

7 Brush with cream 10 minutes before the end of baking time. Leave to cool and slice very thinly.

Pumpernickel – Chicago Style.

1 oz (30 gm) fresh yeast
¼ pint (140 ml) warm water
1 pint (½ litre) warm milk
2 oz (55 gm) margarine
⅛ pint (60 ml) molasses
1 beaten egg
1 teaspoon salt
1½ lb (¾ kg) rye flour
2 tablespoons caraway seeds

Originally from Germany, this recipe transplanted itself along with German immigrants to the mid-West of America in the mid-nineteenth century. It was adapted to suit local taste and the availability of ingredients, and is a firm dark bread that keeps incredibly well and even improves with storing, wrapped in foil. It has a deliciously sweet aroma, and is gorgeous with cheese or hamburger, and a glass of cold beer. In Chicago, it's known as Black Bread.

FIRST STAGE

Dissolve yeast in the liquid and add the sugar. Stir the flours into the yeast mixture until a thick batter is formed. Beat it well with a spoon and put it away to rise for 30 minutes.

SECOND STAGE

1   Blend in the salt, oil, oats and rye flour until a medium soft dough is formed.

2   Knead well for 15 minutes; leave to rise for 1 hour. Knock back dough by kneading.

3   Shape into 2 oval loaves.

4   Punch holes down both sides of the loaves with a floured finger (this will release some of the moisture and prevent stickiness).

5   Leave to prove until the loaves have doubled in size.

6   Bake in a hot oven (425°F, 220°C, Gas 7) for about 1 hour. Brush the loaves with milk or cream about 10 minutes before the end of the baking time.

COUNTRY OATMEAL RYE

Once a favourite throughout the shires of England this is a beautifully moist, dark, country bread, mingled with light flecks of oats. It has a slightly sweet taste, is wholesome, and packed full of protein. Try it with a chunk of cheese and a mug of ale.

FIRST STAGE
1 oz (30 gm) fresh yeast
½ pint (280 ml) warm milk and water
2 oz (50 gm) sugar
1 lb (½ kg) wholemeal flour
1 lb (½ kg) plain white flour

SECOND STAGE
1 teaspoon salt
4 fl oz (110 ml) oil
½ lb (225 gm) oats
½ lb (225 gm) rye flour
milk or cream

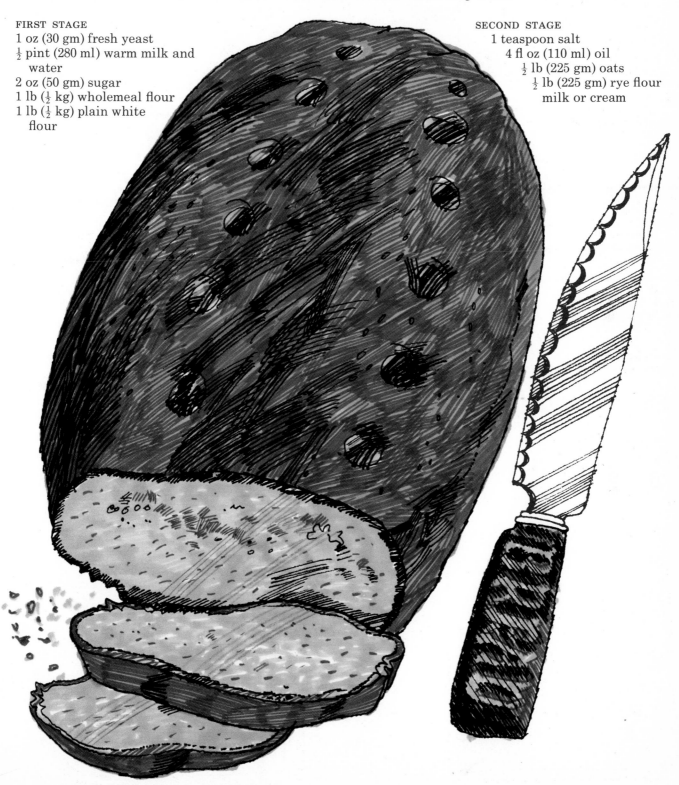

31

1 Dissolve the yeast in some of the warm buttermilk.

2 Add the soda, salt, sugar, and creamed yeast to the remaining buttermilk. Beat well, then gradually add half the flour.

3 Add the melted butter and the rest of the flour.

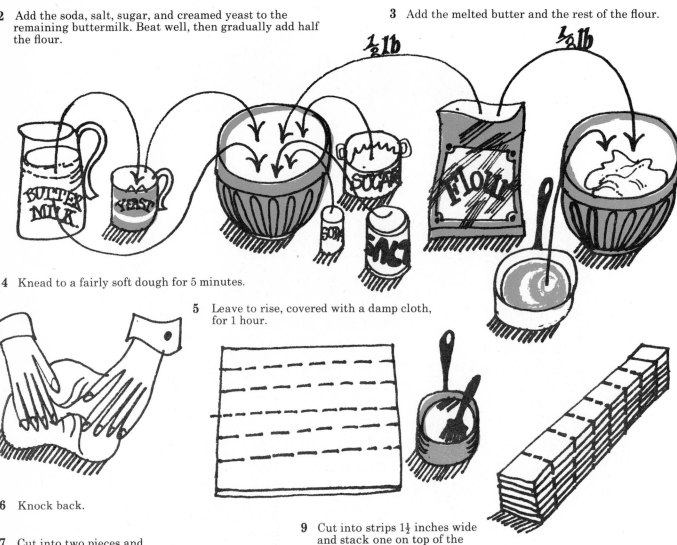

4 Knead to a fairly soft dough for 5 minutes.

5 Leave to rise, covered with a damp cloth, for 1 hour.

6 Knock back.

7 Cut into two pieces and roll each one out to $\frac{1}{8}$ inch thick.

8 Brush both pieces with melted butter.

9 Cut into strips $1\frac{1}{2}$ inches wide and stack one on top of the other, about 6–7 layers. Then, with a sharp knife, cut them into $1\frac{1}{2}$-inch squares.

10 Place them in greased bun-tins, cut side up.

11 Prove in a warm place until doubled, about 1 hour.

12 Bake in a hot oven (425°F, 220°C, Gas 7) for 15–20 minutes.

YANKEE BUTTERMILK ROLLS

This is an old New England favourite, a beautifully soft, golden roll in a decorative shape. The delicious flavour goes with many hot and cold foods, and, as these rolls need not be buttered, they are excellent for buffet parties.

1 oz (30 gm) fresh yeast
1 pint (565 ml) warm buttermilk
¼ teaspoon bicarbonate of soda
1 teaspoon salt
1 oz (30 gm) sugar
1 lb (½ kg) plain flour
1 oz (30 gm) melted butter
1 oz (30 gm) melted butter for brushing

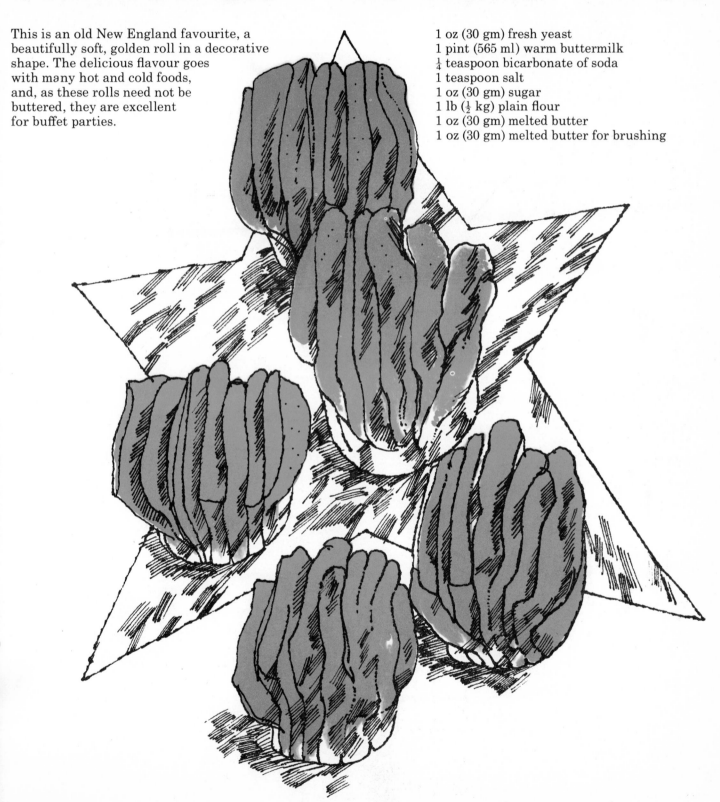

1 Cream the yeast with a little sugar and milk. Put the flour into a bowl and make a well in the centre. Pour the yeast mixture into the well.

2 Add the rest of the milk, melted margarine and salt and mix and knead to a smooth dough. Knead for 10 minutes.

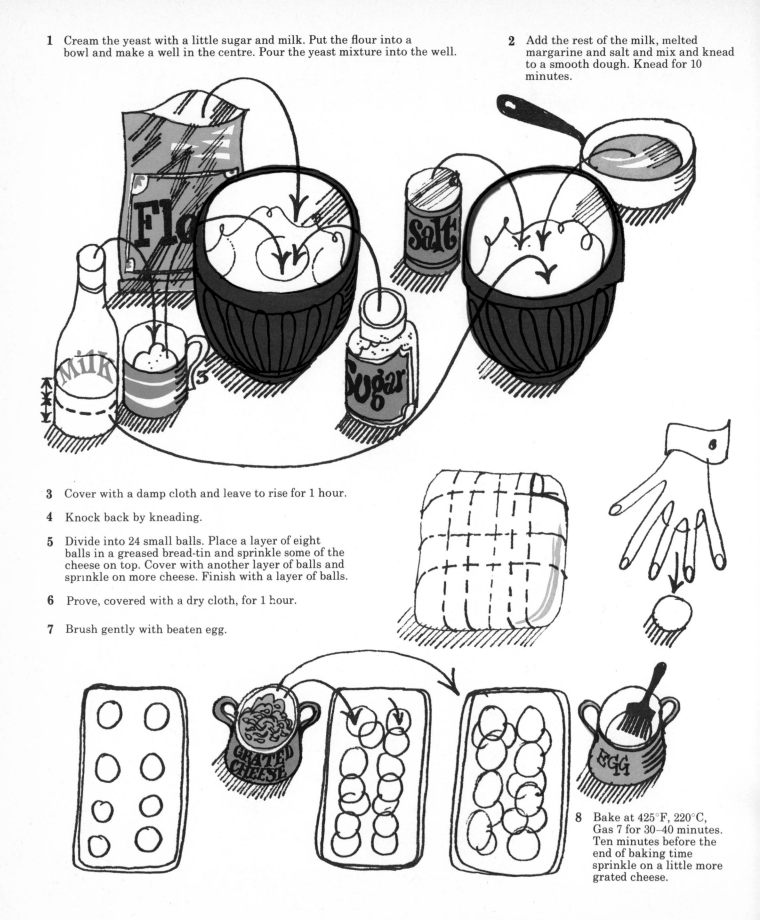

3 Cover with a damp cloth and leave to rise for 1 hour.

4 Knock back by kneading.

5 Divide into 24 small balls. Place a layer of eight balls in a greased bread-tin and sprinkle some of the cheese on top. Cover with another layer of balls and sprinkle on more cheese. Finish with a layer of balls.

6 Prove, covered with a dry cloth, for 1 hour.

7 Brush gently with beaten egg.

8 Bake at 425°F, 220°C, Gas 7 for 30–40 minutes. Ten minutes before the end of baking time sprinkle on a little more grated cheese.

CHEESE BREAD

This rich, golden cheese bread is ideal for picnics, brunch (with a bowl of soup) or an evening snack with a glass of red wine. Full of goodness and nutrition, it also makes an ideal snack for children.

$\frac{1}{2}$ oz (15 gm) fresh yeast
1 teaspoon sugar
$\frac{1}{4}$ pint (140 ml) warm
   milk
8 oz (225 gm) plain
   white flour
2 oz (55 gm) melted
   margarine
$\frac{1}{2}$ teaspoon salt
2 oz (55 gm) grated
   cheese
beaten egg for glaze

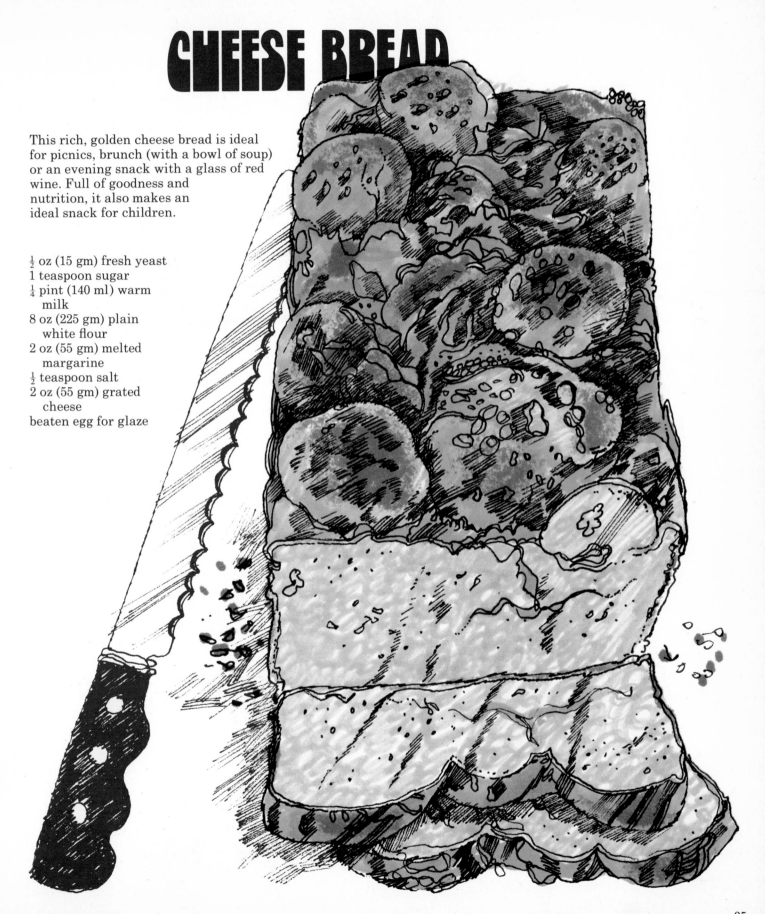

1 Sieve about one-third of the flour into a mixing bowl. Rub in the fresh yeast.

2 Add the sugar and the water and mix to a smooth batter.

3 Cover with a damp cloth and leave to ferment for 15 minutes.

4 Mix the remaining flour and salt into another bowl and rub in the margarine.

5 Combine the batter mixture and the flour mixture to form a fairly soft dough.

6 Knead well, for 10 minutes. Return to bowl, cover with a damp cloth, and leave to rise for about 1 hour.

7 Knock back by kneading, and divide into eight equal portions.

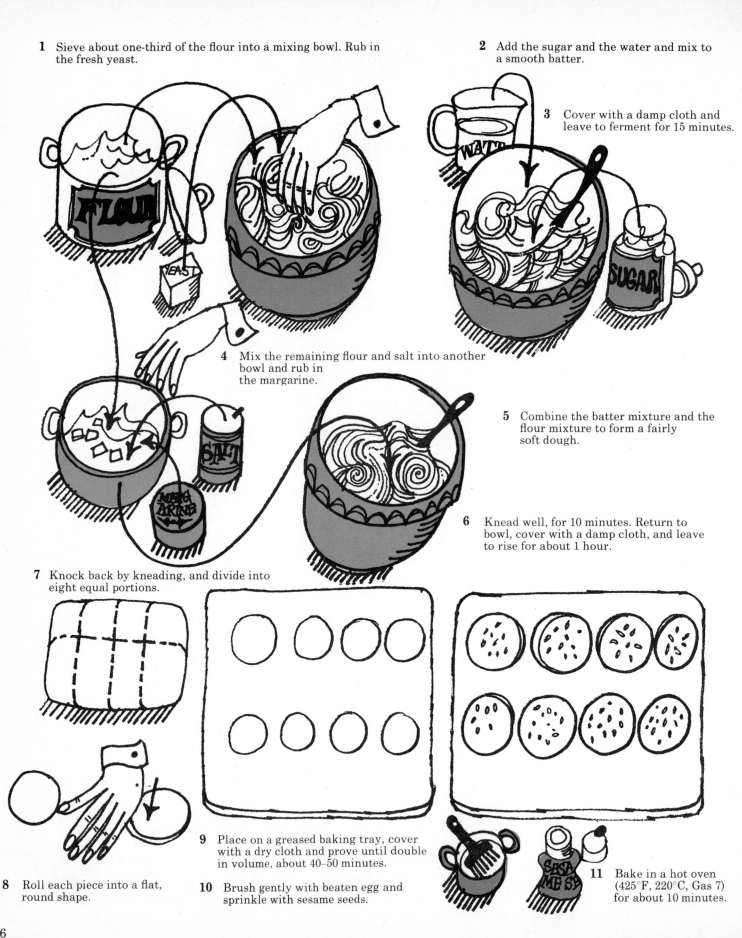

8 Roll each piece into a flat, round shape.

9 Place on a greased baking tray, cover with a dry cloth and prove until double in volume, about 40–50 minutes.

10 Brush gently with beaten egg and sprinkle with sesame seeds.

11 Bake in a hot oven (425°F, 220°C, Gas 7) for about 10 minutes.

THE ALL·AMERICAN HAMBURGER BUN

The hamburger bun, pure and simple, is as American as Thanksgiving and Pumpkin Pie.
It's delicious with a medium-rare minced beef pattie, slices of tomato, gherkins,
ketchup, or sliced onion – wonderful for barbecues and picnics.
Try it with very cold beer.

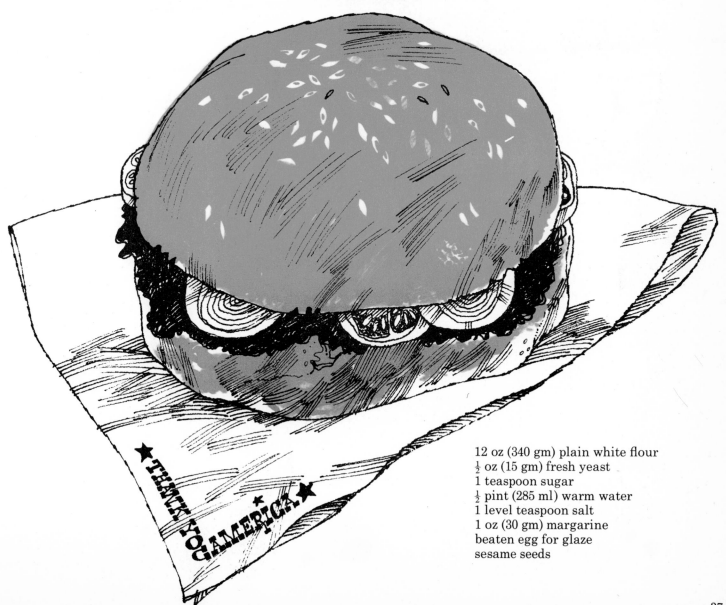

12 oz (340 gm) plain white flour
½ oz (15 gm) fresh yeast
1 teaspoon sugar
½ pint (285 ml) warm water
1 level teaspoon salt
1 oz (30 gm) margarine
beaten egg for glaze
sesame seeds

1 Put the flours and salt into a bowl. Make a well in the centre. Into it pour the Sour Dough Paste, the warm melted fat, the warm milk and the creamed yeast, (page 8).

2 Mix up well.

3 Knead into a smooth, elastic dough for about 15 minutes.

4 Put into a bowl and cover with a damp cloth. Leave to rise in a warm place for 60–90 minutes.

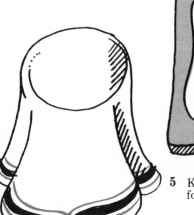

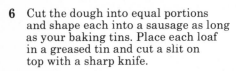

5 Knock back by kneading the dough for a minute.

6 Cut the dough into equal portions and shape each into a sausage as long as your baking tins. Place each loaf in a greased tin and cut a slit on top with a sharp knife.

7 Bake the loaves in a hot oven (425°F, 220°C, Gas 7) for 30 minutes. Then remove from oven and brush them with cream or evaporated milk to give them a glossy finish. Put back into a cooler oven (350°F, 180°C, Gas 4) for at least another hour and a half.

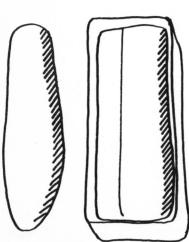

8 Now you have a real Westphalian Sour Dough Rye with a traditional shine.

Westphalian Sour Dough Rye

This rye bread, which is a favourite throughout the Upper Rhine, has a firm smooth texture, making it ideal for picnics and cookouts. Usually eaten with Westphalian ham and a mug of beer, it adds gusto to any party.

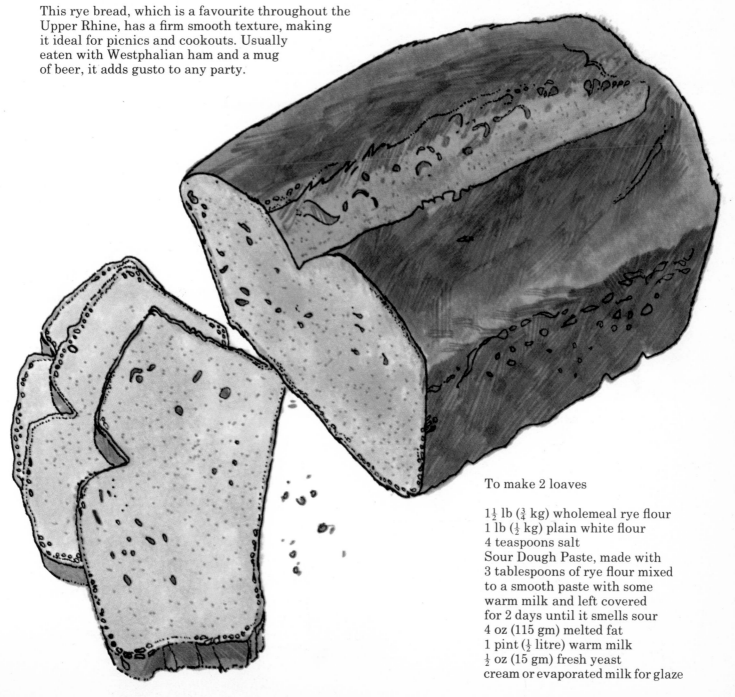

To make 2 loaves

1½ lb (¾ kg) wholemeal rye flour
1 lb (½ kg) plain white flour
4 teaspoons salt
Sour Dough Paste, made with
3 tablespoons of rye flour mixed
to a smooth paste with some
warm milk and left covered
for 2 days until it smells sour
4 oz (115 gm) melted fat
1 pint (½ litre) warm milk
½ oz (15 gm) fresh yeast
cream or evaporated milk for glaze

1 Put oats into a bowl, pour on milk and leave to soak for at least 2 hours.

2 Add to the oats the creamed yeast (page 8), melted margarine, salt, and enough flour to make a nice smooth dough.

3/4

3 Knead for 10 minutes.

4 Leave to rise, covered with a damp cloth, for about 1 hour.

5 Knock back by kneading.

6 Shape into 16 buns and cut across the tops with a sharp knife or kitchen scissors.

7 Prove on a greased baking sheet until doubled in size.

8 Brush gently with cream or beaten egg. Bake in a hot oven (425°F, 220°C, Gas 7) for about 20 minutes.

North of the Border Oatmeal Rolls

Deliciously moist rolls which have the taste of real oatmeal, are golden brown in colour, and have a rough, moist texture; they are ideal as an accompaniment to soups, fish and creamy hors d'oeuvres. Try them for lunch on a cold winter's day with a bowl of Scotch Broth.

8 oz (225 gm) oats
¾ pint (425 ml) milk
½ oz (15 gm) fresh yeast

2 oz (55 gm) melted margarine
1 teaspoon salt
8 oz (225 gm) plain white flour
cream or beaten egg for glaze

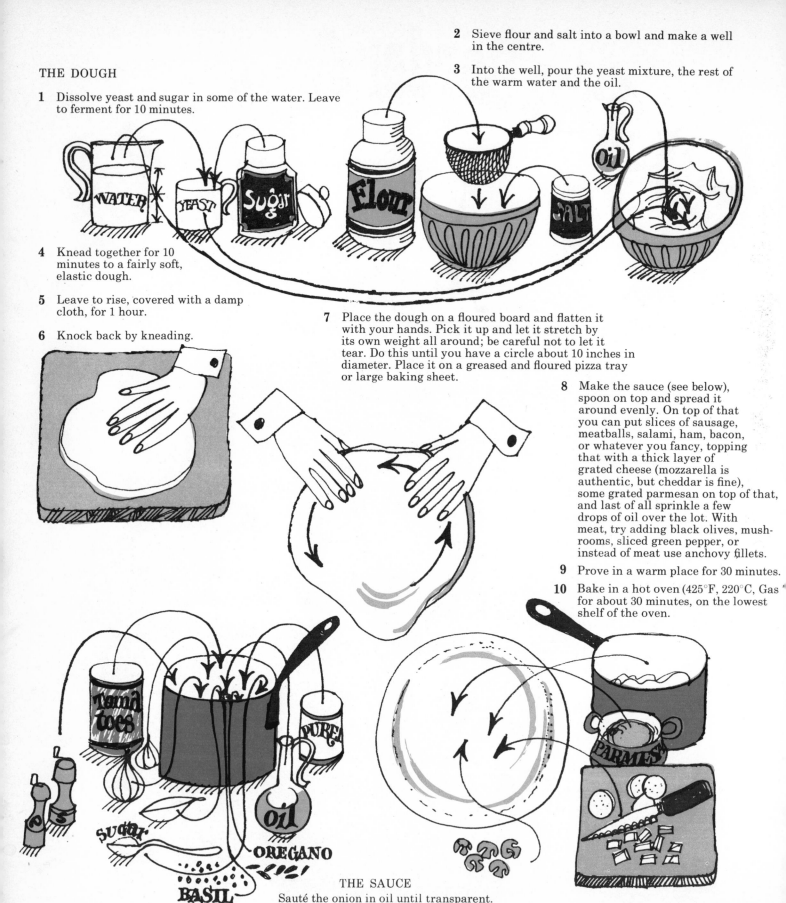

THE DOUGH

1 Dissolve yeast and sugar in some of the water. Leave to ferment for 10 minutes.

2 Sieve flour and salt into a bowl and make a well in the centre.

3 Into the well, pour the yeast mixture, the rest of the warm water and the oil.

4 Knead together for 10 minutes to a fairly soft, elastic dough.

5 Leave to rise, covered with a damp cloth, for 1 hour.

6 Knock back by kneading.

7 Place the dough on a floured board and flatten it with your hands. Pick it up and let it stretch by its own weight all around; be careful not to let it tear. Do this until you have a circle about 10 inches in diameter. Place it on a greased and floured pizza tray or large baking sheet.

8 Make the sauce (see below), spoon on top and spread it around evenly. On top of that you can put slices of sausage, meatballs, salami, ham, bacon, or whatever you fancy, topping that with a thick layer of grated cheese (mozzarella is authentic, but cheddar is fine), some grated parmesan on top of that, and last of all sprinkle a few drops of oil over the lot. With meat, try adding black olives, mushrooms, sliced green pepper, or instead of meat use anchovy fillets.

9 Prove in a warm place for 30 minutes.

10 Bake in a hot oven (425°F, 220°C, Gas for about 30 minutes, on the lowest shelf of the oven.

THE SAUCE

Sauté the onion in oil until transparent. Add crushed clove of garlic and fry a further 1 minute. Add tin of tomatoes and break them up slightly, the tomato purée, bay leaf, sugar, salt, pepper, oregano and basil. Simmer gently, partially covered, for about 1 hour. The sauce should be quite thick and is then ready for use (cool a little first). You can strain the sauce if you wish.

PIZZA

Enjoy the taste of genuine
Italian cooking with this
truly beautiful Italian Pizza –
typically juicy, meaty and a
delight to the palate.
Try it with a glass of Chianti,
laughter and good conversation.
Ideal for parties, or even a late,
late night snack.

THE DOUGH
½ oz (15 gm) fresh yeast
1 teaspoon sugar
¼ pint (140 ml) warm
 water
8 oz (225 gm) plain white
 flour
1 teaspoon salt
5 tablespoons oil

THE SAUCE
large chopped onion
oil for frying
1 clove garlic
15 oz (425 gm) tin tomatoes
small tin tomato purée
1 bay leaf
1 teaspoon sugar
1 teaspoon salt
¼ teaspoon pepper
1 teaspoon oregano
1 teaspoon basil

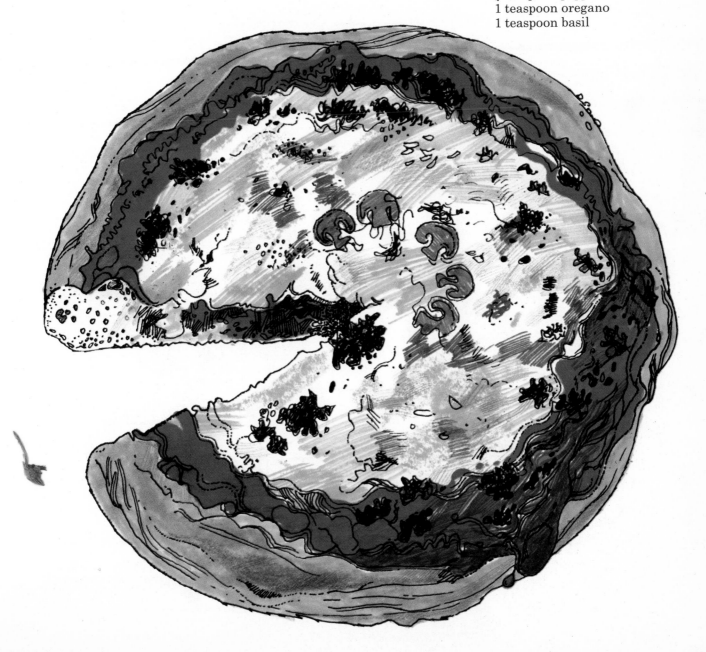

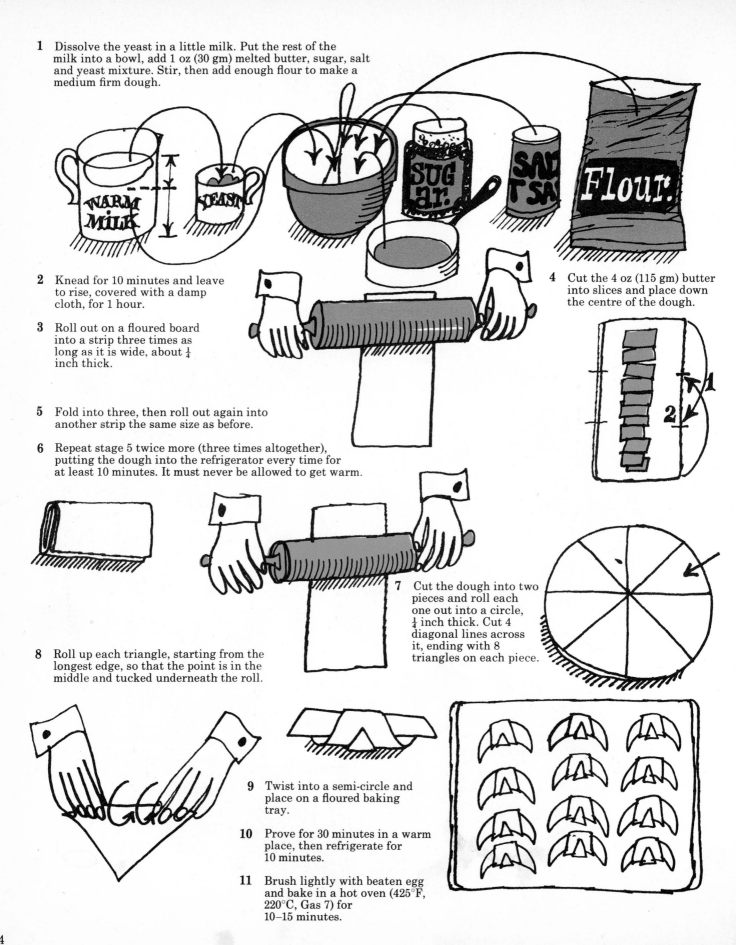

1 Dissolve the yeast in a little milk. Put the rest of the milk into a bowl, add 1 oz (30 gm) melted butter, sugar, salt and yeast mixture. Stir, then add enough flour to make a medium firm dough.

2 Knead for 10 minutes and leave to rise, covered with a damp cloth, for 1 hour.

3 Roll out on a floured board into a strip three times as long as it is wide, about $\frac{1}{4}$ inch thick.

4 Cut the 4 oz (115 gm) butter into slices and place down the centre of the dough.

5 Fold into three, then roll out again into another strip the same size as before.

6 Repeat stage 5 twice more (three times altogether), putting the dough into the refrigerator every time for at least 10 minutes. It must never be allowed to get warm.

7 Cut the dough into two pieces and roll each one out into a circle, $\frac{1}{4}$ inch thick. Cut 4 diagonal lines across it, ending with 8 triangles on each piece.

8 Roll up each triangle, starting from the longest edge, so that the point is in the middle and tucked underneath the roll.

9 Twist into a semi-circle and place on a floured baking tray.

10 Prove for 30 minutes in a warm place, then refrigerate for 10 minutes.

11 Brush lightly with beaten egg and bake in a hot oven (425°F, 220°C, Gas 7) for 10–15 minutes.

CROISSANTS

A delicate, feather-light, breakfast
roll that should always be eaten
hot. Croissants are light, buttery
rolls sacred to the French breakfast
table; they add distinction to
any breakfast, and are a must with
good hot coffee. Bon jour!

1 oz (30 gm) fresh yeast
¼ pint (140 ml) warm milk
1 oz (30 gm) melted butter
1 teaspoon sugar
1 teaspoon salt
12 oz (340 gm) plain white flour
4 oz (115 gm) butter
beaten egg for glaze

1 Sieve the flour and salt into a bowl. Make two wells in it.

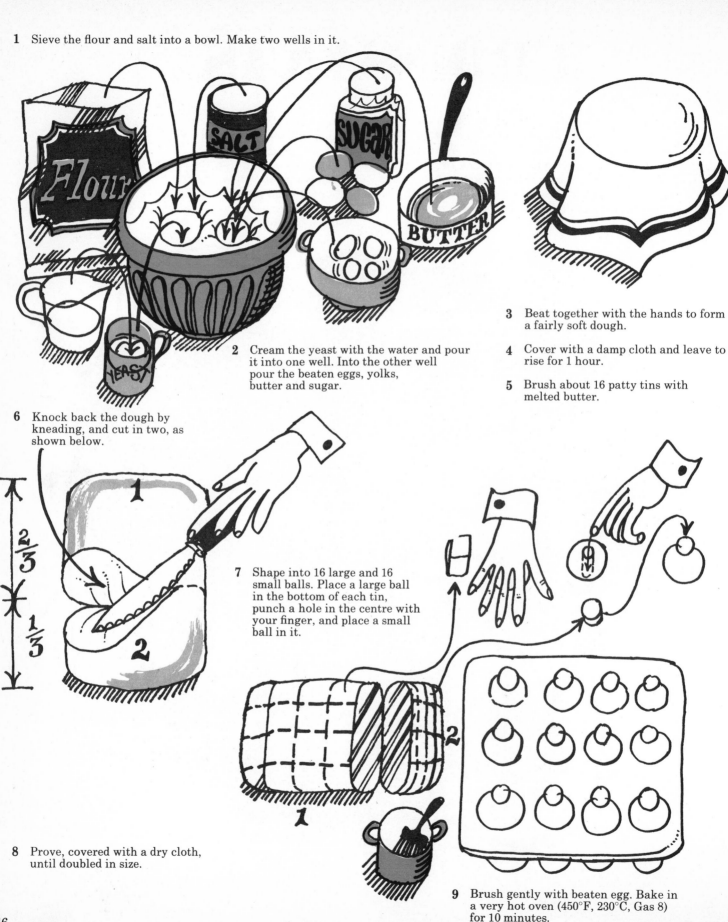

2 Cream the yeast with the water and pour it into one well. Into the other well pour the beaten eggs, yolks, butter and sugar.

3 Beat together with the hands to form a fairly soft dough.

4 Cover with a damp cloth and leave to rise for 1 hour.

5 Brush about 16 patty tins with melted butter.

6 Knock back the dough by kneading, and cut in two, as shown below.

7 Shape into 16 large and 16 small balls. Place a large ball in the bottom of each tin, punch a hole in the centre with your finger, and place a small ball in it.

8 Prove, covered with a dry cloth, until doubled in size.

9 Brush gently with beaten egg. Bake in a very hot oven (450°F, 230°C, Gas 8) for 10 minutes.

46

BRIOCHES

A slightly sweet roll from France, brioches are a typical and quite delicious part of a French breakfast. Eat brioche rolls fresh and wash them down with steaming cups of coffee – a real treat to start a leisurely day. The unique shape lends distinction and style to any breakfast table.

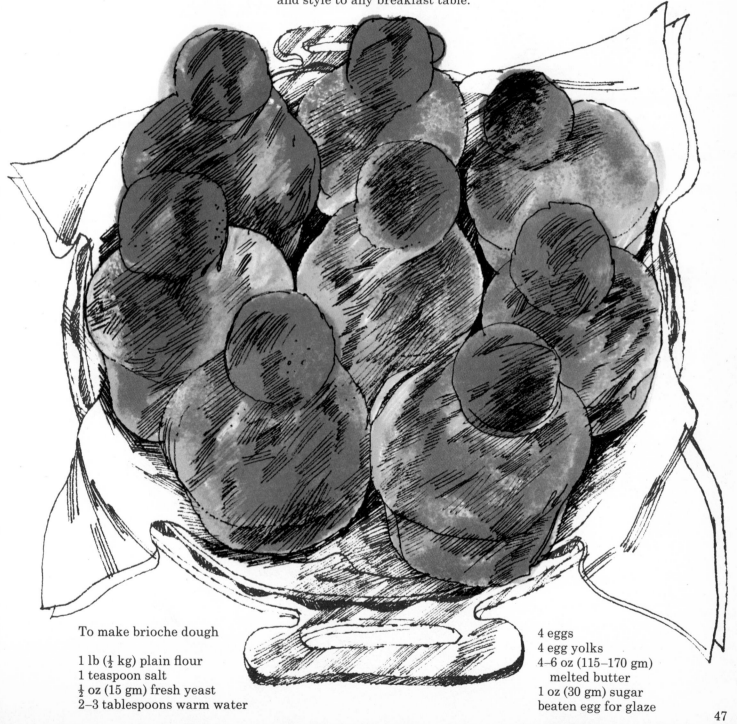

To make brioche dough

1 lb (½ kg) plain flour
1 teaspoon salt
½ oz (15 gm) fresh yeast
2–3 tablespoons warm water

4 eggs
4 egg yolks
4–6 oz (115–170 gm)
　melted butter
1 oz (30 gm) sugar
beaten egg for glaze

1 Dissolve the yeast in a little of the water.

2 Sieve the flour and salt into a bowl, make a well in the centre and pour the yeast into it. Add 1 oz flaked lard and the rest of the water.

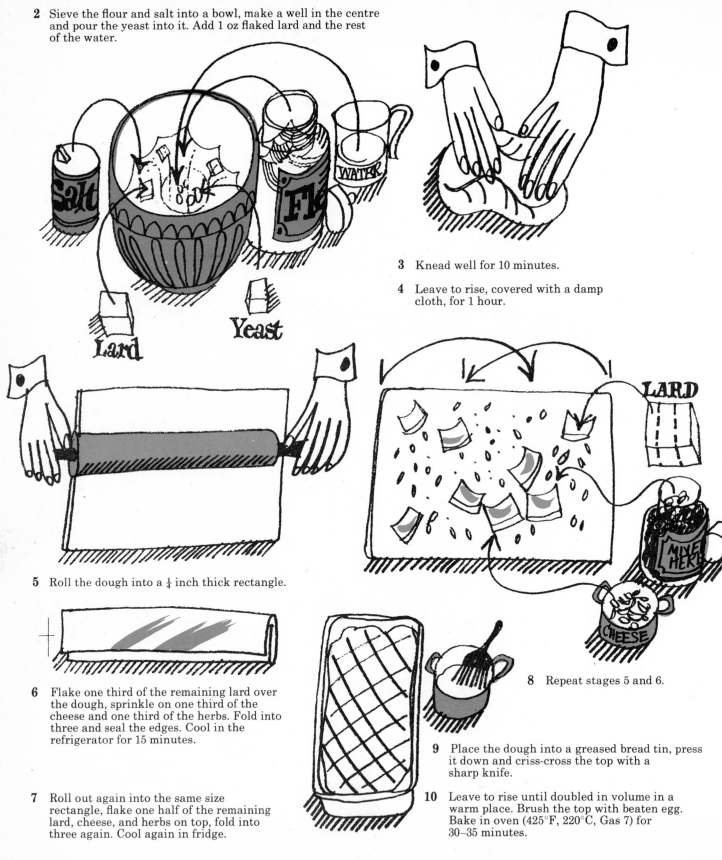

3 Knead well for 10 minutes.

4 Leave to rise, covered with a damp cloth, for 1 hour.

5 Roll the dough into a ¼ inch thick rectangle.

6 Flake one third of the remaining lard over the dough, sprinkle on one third of the cheese and one third of the herbs. Fold into three and seal the edges. Cool in the refrigerator for 15 minutes.

7 Roll out again into the same size rectangle, flake one half of the remaining lard, cheese, and herbs on top, fold into three again. Cool again in fridge.

8 Repeat stages 5 and 6.

9 Place the dough into a greased bread tin, press it down and criss-cross the top with a sharp knife.

10 Leave to rise until doubled in volume in a warm place. Brush the top with beaten egg. Bake in oven (425°F, 220°C, Gas 7) for 30–35 minutes.

Old English Herb Bread.

A soft centred, crusty bread to which layers of cheese and herbs give a unique character and flavour. Its savoury quality makes it ideal for a quick and nourishing lunch – eat it with a bowl of hot soup. It is great for parties too – re-heat it and serve it hot!

½ oz (15 gm) fresh yeast
½ pint (¼ litre) warm water
1 lb (½ kg) plain white flour
1 teaspoon salt

3 oz (85 gm) lard
6 oz (170 gm) grated Cheddar
2 teaspoons mixed herbs
beaten egg for glaze

(or try it with 4 oz (115 gm) cheese and 1 lb (½ kg) finely sliced,.cooked onion)

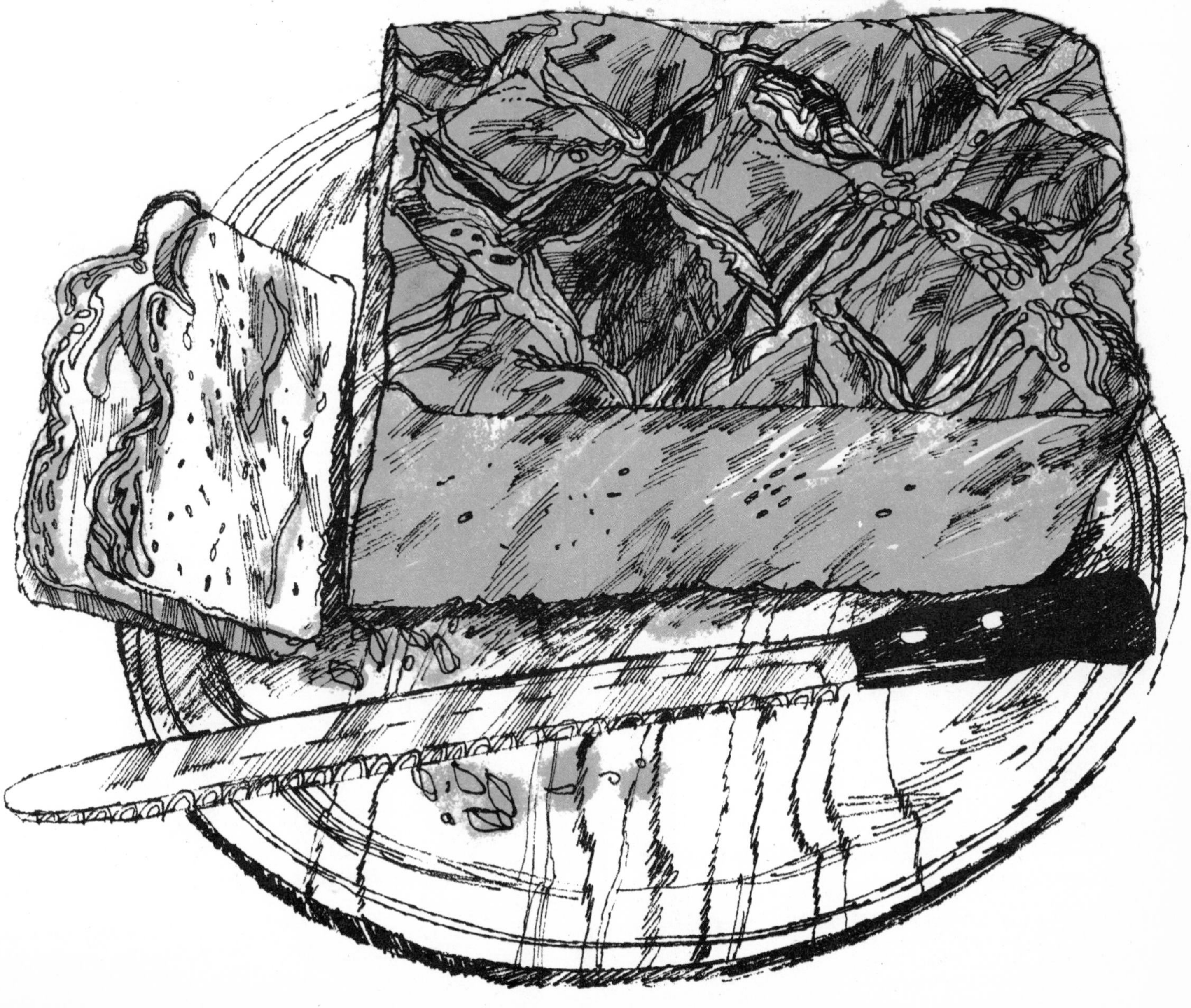

1 Sieve the flour and salt into a bowl. Add the grated rind of orange (if used) and the raisins and the sugar.

2 Cream the yeast with 1 teaspoon sugar and warm milk and add the beaten egg to it.

4 Mix and knead well, for at least 10 minutes. Leave to rise in a warm place, covered with damp cloth, for 60–90 minutes. Knock back the dough by kneading. Divide into three equal portions.

3 Pour the mixture into a well in the flour, add the rest of the warm milk and melted fat.

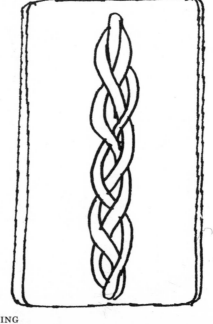

5 Roll each piece into a long strand, about 15 inches long. Dampen the tops and press them together. Plait.

6 Put the loaf on a greased baking tray and leave to prove, covered with a dry cloth, until doubled in size.

TOPPING

7 Bake in a hot oven (425°F, 220°C Gas 7) for 15 minutes. Remove and brush with beaten egg or cream. Put back into a cooler oven (325°F, 170°C, Gas 3) for 30–35 minutes.

8 When cool, mix up icing sugar and warm water thick enough to coat the back of a spoon heavily, then dribble all over loaf. Sprinkle toasted almonds and glacé cherry bits over icing quickly, before it has time to set.

Harvest Festival Raisin Bread

This magnificent fruity sweet bread will tempt one and all. Spread it with just a little butter and you have the perfect prelude to morning coffee.

1 lb ($\frac{1}{2}$ kg) plain white
  flour
$\frac{1}{2}$ teaspoon salt
coarsely grated rind of
  1 orange (optional)
4 oz (115 gm) seedless
  raisins
1 oz (30 gm) sugar
$\frac{1}{2}$ oz (15 gm) fresh yeast
1 teaspoon sugar
$\frac{1}{3}$ pint (170 ml) warm milk
1 egg, beaten
2 oz (55 gm) melted fat
beaten egg or cream for
  glaze

TOPPING
3 oz (85 gm) icing sugar
a little warm water
toasted, flaked almonds
chopped glacé cherries

1 Cream the butter, egg yolks, sugar and vanilla until fluffy.

2 Add the yeast, creamed with a little of the warm milk, and alternately milk, flour, raisins and lemon peel, and beat well until the dough forms bubbles.

3 Now add the beaten egg whites. The dough should be quite soft.

4 Pour the mixture into a greased and floured mould.

5 Prove in a warm place for 1 hour, covered with a dry cloth.

6 Bake at medium heat (375°F, 190°C, Gas 5) for about 1 hour. Cool and dust heavily with icing sugar.

VIENNESE GUGELHUPF

Gugelhupf is a traditional Austrian cake, which has been a favourite with Viennese society since the glorious days of the Empire. It was a favourite indulgence of Emperor Franz Josef I. You'll find its distinctive shape in any of the great coffee-houses all over Austria. Try it with a cup of hot coffee, topped with whipped cream – and you have an authentic 'Austrian Jause' (afternoon coffee).

4 oz (115 gm) butter
4 egg yolks
5 oz (140 gm) caster sugar
vanilla essence
1 oz (30 gm) fresh yeast
¼ pint (140 ml) warm milk

1 lb (½ kg) plain white flour
4 oz (115 gm) raisins
lemon peel (optional)
2 egg whites
icing sugar for dusting

1 Sieve $\frac{1}{3}$ of the flour into a bowl. Rub in the fresh yeast. Add 1 teaspoon sugar and all the milk; mix up well. Cover with a damp cloth and leave to ferment for 15 minutes.

2 Sieve the remaining flour and sugar and salt into another bowl. Rub in the margarine.

3 Add the flour mixture with the beaten egg to the yeast mixture and knead it all to a fairly soft, elastic dough.

4 Cover with a damp cloth and leave to rise for 1 hour.

5 Knock back by kneading.

6 Roll the dough out into an oblong about 10 × 12 inches.

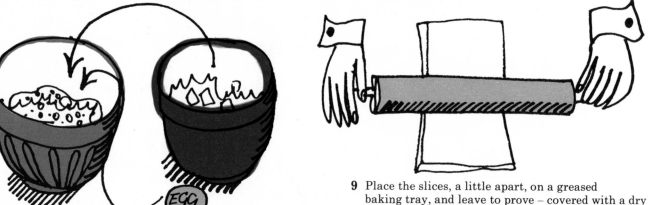

9 Place the slices, a little apart, on a greased baking tray, and leave to prove – covered with a dry cloth – for about 40 minutes. Bake in a hot oven (425°F, 220°C, Gas 7) for 20 minutes.

7 Brush about 1 oz of melted margarine, on top, sprinkle on 3 tablespoons of caster sugar, 3 tablespoons currants, and 1 teaspoon of mixed spice.

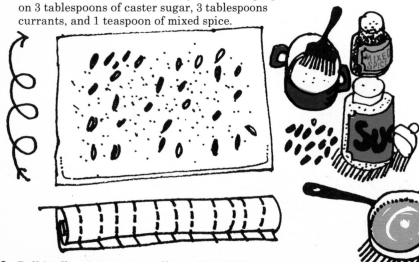

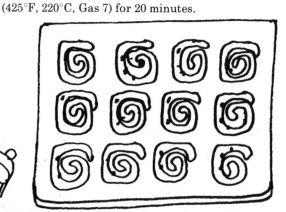

THE GLAZE: Heat the sugar and water over low heat until all the sugar has dissolved. Bring it to a boil and boil rapidly without stirring for 1–2 minutes, until the syrup thickens. Brush buns with the syrup while they are still warm, and immediately sprinkle a little caster sugar on each one.

8 Roll it all up into a neat roll, starting at the longest side. With a sharp knife cut the roll into 12 equal slices.

THE CHELSEA BUN

The Chelsea Bun is a traditional favourite throughout England.
With a beautifully sweet, fruity taste, it makes an ideal accompaniment to coffee or tea,
and is frequently an indulgence of those who should not indulge.
Mr. Pickwick would have loved them.

10 oz (280 gm) plain flour
$\frac{1}{2}$ oz (13 gm) fresh yeast
1 oz (25 gm) sugar
$\frac{1}{4}$ pint (140 ml) warm milk
$\frac{1}{2}$ teaspoon salt
2 oz (50 gm) margarine
1 beaten egg
1 oz melted margarine
3 tablespoons caster sugar
3 tablespoons currants
1 teaspoon mixed spice

SUGAR GLAZE
2 tablespoons sugar
3 tablespoons water

1 Mix the yeast with a little warm milk and a teaspoon of sugar.

2 Rub the lard into the flour and mix in all the dry ingredients.

currents

3 Make a well in the centre and add the yeast mixture and the egg.

4 Mix to a soft dough with a little more warm milk.

5 Knead well for about 10 minutes.

6 Leave to rise, covered with a damp cloth, for 1½ hours. Knock back by kneading.

7 Put into a well greased loaf tin. Prove until double in bulk, covered with a dry cloth. Bake at 375°F, 190°C, Gas 5, for 1½ to 2 hours. Brush with sugar glaze (see below) while still hot.

THE GLAZE: Dissolve 2 tablespoons of sugar in 3 tablespoons of warm water. Bring to boil and boil rapidly for a minute, until the syrup thickens. Use immediately.

BARA BRITH

A traditional, rich, Welsh, spicy, sweet bread. Thickly spread with butter, it is delicious with an afternoon cup of tea, a warm hearth, and a little friendly gossip.

1 oz (30 gm) fresh yeast
a little warm milk
1 teaspoon sugar
4 oz (115 gm) lard or butter
1 lb (½ kg) plain flour
4 oz (115 gm) sultanas
1 oz (30 gm) mixed peel
¼ teaspoon mixed spice
4 oz (115 gm) brown sugar
½ teaspoon salt
4 oz (115 gm) raisins
4 oz (115 gm) currants
1 egg
warm milk to mix

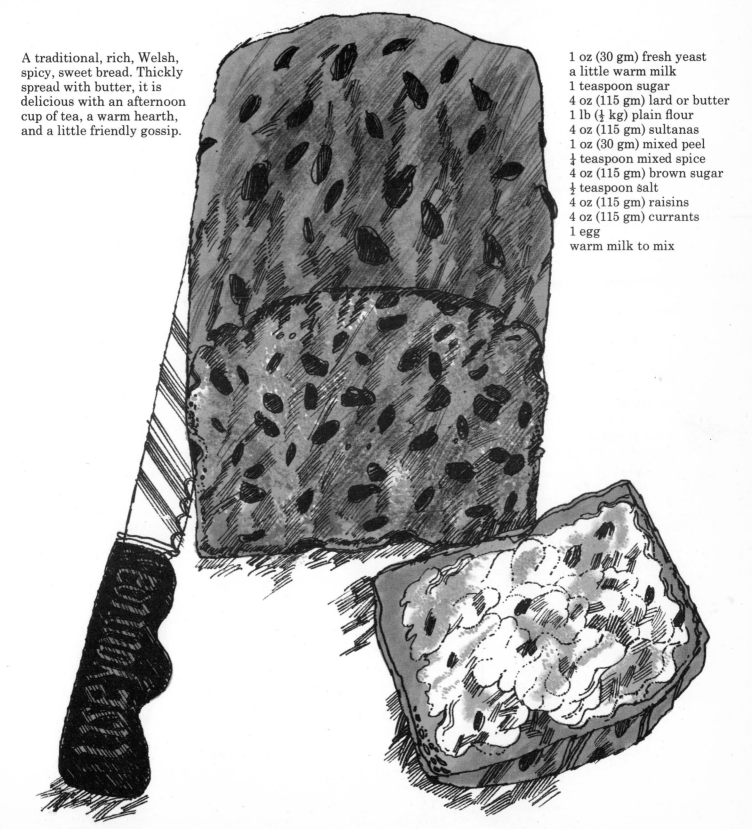

Work with cold ingredients and cool hands on a cold surface.

1 Sieve flour and salt into a bowl and rub in lard.

2 Add some of the water to yeast, and cream. Mix together sugar and egg and add to yeast.

3 Make a well in the flour, pour in the yeast mixture, and mix with the rest of the water until a fairly soft dough is formed. Beat well until smooth.

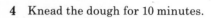

4 Knead the dough for 10 minutes.

5 Roll out into a square.

7 Roll out lengthwise again, repeat folding as for stage 6. Repeat stage 6 once more. After each process place dough in refrigerator for 15 minutes. Never let the dough get warm.

6 Put slices of butter all down the centre. Fold three times and roll out lengthwise. Fold again three times and give ½ turn.

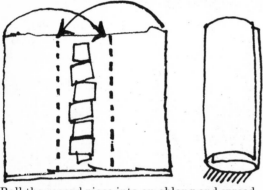

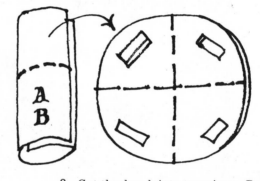

9 Roll the second piece into an oblong and spread it with the butter, creamed with the sugar and cinnamon. Sprinkle sultanas and peel on top. Cut into two pieces lengthwise.

10 Roll up one half, cut into 4 slices, flatten these slightly, and place on a baking tray.

8 Cut the dough into two pieces. Roll one piece into a circle, and cut into quarters. Put a small piece of almond paste on widest point of triangle, moisten straight sides, and roll up from the widest point so that the point is outside and under the roll. Make into a croissant shape.

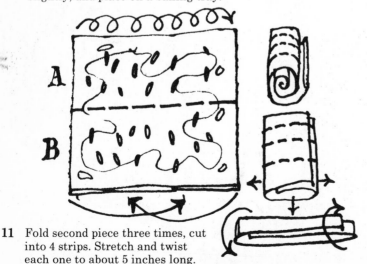

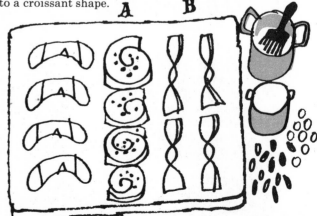

11 Fold second piece three times, cut into 4 strips. Stretch and twist each one to about 5 inches long. Place on tray. Leave to prove in a warm place, covered with a dry cloth, about 30 minutes. Put into refrigerator for 15 minutes before placing in oven.

12 Brush them gently with beaten egg. Bake at 425°F, 220°C, Gas 7 for 12–15 minutes. When cooled, drizzle on the icing (icing sugar mixed with a little bit of water to make it *just* runny). Decorate with chopped nuts, chopped almonds and chopped cherries.

DANISH PASTRY

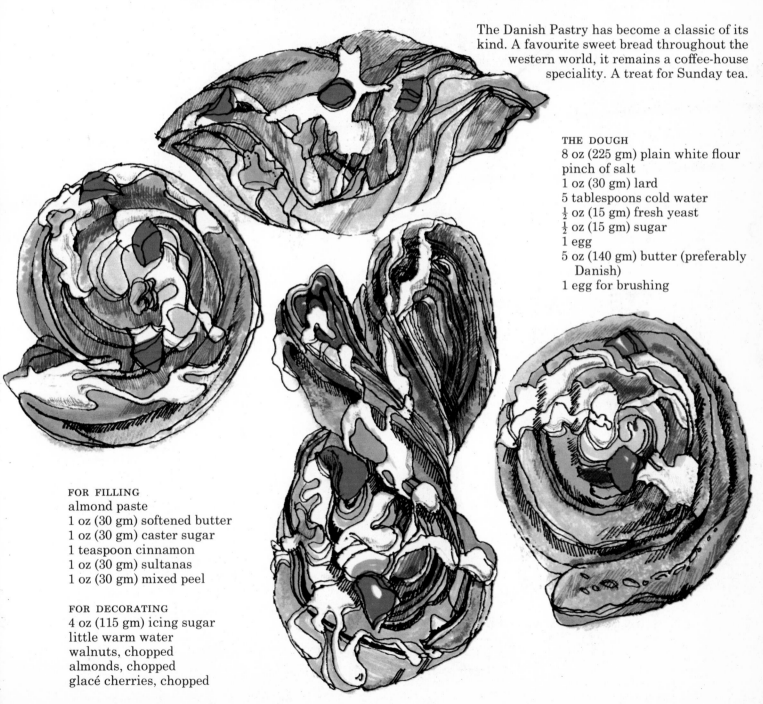

The Danish Pastry has become a classic of its kind. A favourite sweet bread throughout the western world, it remains a coffee-house speciality. A treat for Sunday tea.

THE DOUGH
8 oz (225 gm) plain white flour
pinch of salt
1 oz (30 gm) lard
5 tablespoons cold water
½ oz (15 gm) fresh yeast
½ oz (15 gm) sugar
1 egg
5 oz (140 gm) butter (preferably Danish)
1 egg for brushing

FOR FILLING
almond paste
1 oz (30 gm) softened butter
1 oz (30 gm) caster sugar
1 teaspoon cinnamon
1 oz (30 gm) sultanas
1 oz (30 gm) mixed peel

FOR DECORATING
4 oz (115 gm) icing sugar
little warm water
walnuts, chopped
almonds, chopped
glacé cherries, chopped

1 Cream the yeast with a little warm water.

2 Sieve the flour and salt into a bowl, add the yeast mixture and enough water to form a fairly firm dough.

3 Knead for 5–10 minutes.

4 Leave to rise, covered with a damp cloth, for 1 hour.

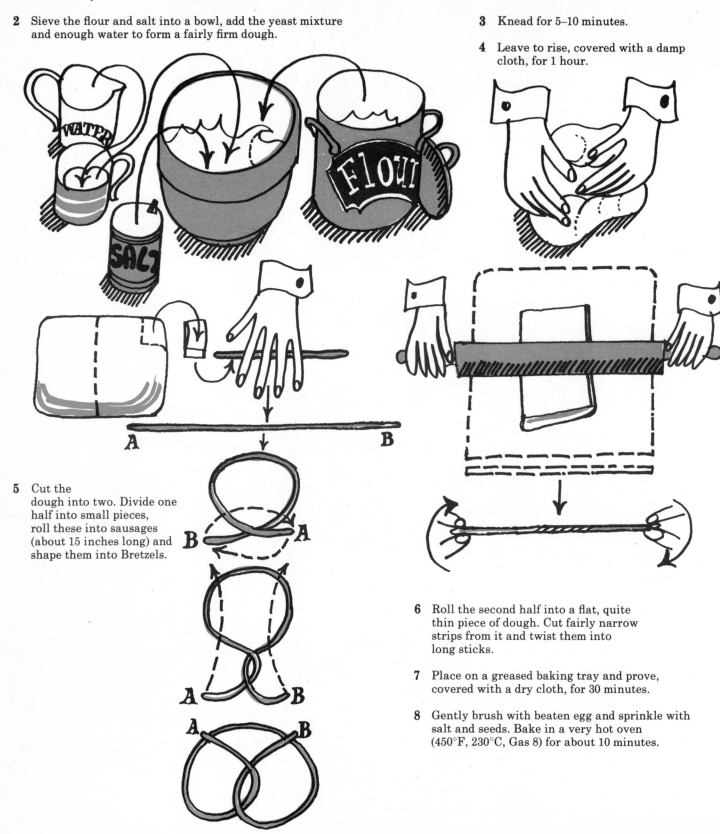

5 Cut the dough into two. Divide one half into small pieces, roll these into sausages (about 15 inches long) and shape them into Bretzels.

6 Roll the second half into a flat, quite thin piece of dough. Cut fairly narrow strips from it and twist them into long sticks.

7 Place on a greased baking tray and prove, covered with a dry cloth, for 30 minutes.

8 Gently brush with beaten egg and sprinkle with salt and seeds. Bake in a very hot oven (450°F, 230°C, Gas 8) for about 10 minutes.

Salzstangen and Bretzeln

This is an original 19th century German recipe. Crisp and crunchy favourites at cocktail parties, the delicate, ornamental shapes and the glowing, golden colours enhance any snack tray. These go especially well with cold beer.

½ oz (15 gm) fresh yeast
approx. ½ cup warm water
8 oz (225 gm) plain flour
½ teaspoon salt
1 egg for glaze
salt
poppy seeds
caraway seeds
sesame seeds

Index

B

baking 9
Bara Brith 56–7
beer with
    French Loaf 13
    Saltzstangen and Bretzeln 61
black bread, Pumpernickel 28–9
breads
    Cheese 34–5
    Grandmama's Milk 18–19
    Harvest Festival Raisin 50–1
    Monastery Oatmeal 24–5
    Old English Herb 48–9
    Poppy Seed 22–3
breakfast
    Brioche Rolls 46–7
    Croissant Rolls 44–5
    Monastery Oatmeal Bread 24–5
    Poppy Seed Bread 22–3
Bretzeln, Saltzstangen and 60–1
Brioches 46–7
Bun, The All-American
    Hamburger 36–7
Buns, Chelsea 54–5

C

Cheese Bread 34–5
cheese with
    Cottage Loaf 15
    Country Oatmeal Rye 31
    French Country Loaf 21
    French Loaf 13
Chelsea Buns 54–5
chianti with Pizza 43
children's snack, Cheese Bread
    34–5
coffee with Viennese Gugelhupf
    53
Cottage Loaf, The 14–15
Country Oatmeal Rye 30–1
Croissants 44–5
crusty loaves
    Monastery Oatmeal 24–5
    Old English Farmhouse 10–11
    Old English Herb 48–9

D

Danish Pastries 58–9
Dinner Rolls 16–17

E

English
    Chelsea Buns 54–5
    Country Oatmeal Rye 30–1
    Farmhouse Loaf 10–11
    Herb Bread 48–9

F

Farmhouse Loaf, English 10–11
fish, with North of the Border
    Oatmeal Rolls 41
French
    Brioches 41–2
    Country Loaf 20–1
    Croissants 44–5
    Loaf 12–13
fruity bread
    Chelsea Buns 54–5
    Harvest Festival Raisin Bread
    50–1

G

German, Saltzstangen and
    Bretzeln 60–1
glazes 9
Grandmama's Milk Bread 18–19
Gugelhupf, Viennese 52–3

H

ham, with Westphalian Sour
    Dough Rye 39
Harvest Festival Raisin Bread
    50–1
Herb Bread, Old English 48–9
honey, with Monastery Oatmeal
    Bread 25
hors-d'oeuvres, with North of the
    Border Oatmeal Rolls 41

I, K

Italian Pizza 42–3
kneading 8
knocking back 8

L

loaves
    Cottage 14–15
    French, The 12–13
    French Country 20–1
    Old English Farmhouse 10–11

M, N

Milk Bread, Grandmama's 18–19
Monastery Oatmeal Bread 24–5
North of the Border Oatmeal
    Rolls 40–1

O

Oatmeal
    Bread, Monastery 24–5
    North of the Border Rolls 40–1
    Rye, Country 30–1
Old English Herb Bread 48–9

P

Pastries, Danish 58–9
Pizza 42–3
Poppy Seed Bread 22–3
port with Cottage Loaf 15
proving 8
Pumpernickel – Chicago Style
    28–9

R

re-heating 9
rising 8
rolls
    Brioches 46–7
    Croissants 44–5
    Dinner 16–17
    North of the Border Oatmeal
    40–1
    Yankee Buttermilk 32–3
Rye
    Country Oatmeal 30–1
    Westphalian Sour Dough 38–9

S

Saltztangen and Bretzeln 60–1
sandwiches, Grandmama's Milk
    Bread 19
savoury bread, Old English Herb
    Bread 49
soup with
    Cheese Bread 35
    North of the Border Oatmeal
    Rolls 41
    Old English Herb Bread 49
Sour Dough Rye, Westphalian
    38–9
sweet breads
    Bara Brith 56–7
    Danish Pastries 58–9
    Poppy Seed Bread 22–3

V

Vienna Bread 26–7
Viennese Gugelhupf 52–3

W

Welsh, Bara Brith 57
Westphalian Sour Dough Rye
    38–9
Wholemeal, Cottage Loaf 15
Wiener Schnitzel, Vienna Bread
    with 27

Y

Yankee Buttermilk Rolls 32–3
yeast 8